Protestant Pulse

Protestant Pulse

Heart Hopes for God

Sharon R. Chace

RESOURCE *Publications* • Eugene, Oregon

PROTESTANT PULSE
Heart Hopes for God

Resource Publications
An Imprint of Wipf and Stock Publishers
199 W. 8th Ave., Suite 3
Eugene, OR 97401

www.wipfandstock.com

ISBN 13: 978-1-60608-705-3

Manufactured in the U.S.A.

This book is dedicated to my husband, Ernest, and our daughter, Amy Elizabeth, who as a teenager said when I faced a rejected manuscript, "Mom, I want you to know that life is going to turn out all right."

Contents

Acknowledgments

My husband, Ernest, and daughter, Amy, are cheerleaders. I am grateful for their enthusiasm. Thank you to Martin E. Marty and John W. O'Malley, SJ, who, as church and cultural historians, have been especially interested in my exploration of the ways that art intersects with religion. During my semester at Yale Divinity School, Leander E. Keck and Christopher R. Seitz encouraged painterly exegesis. Another supporter of my artistic interests, Lorine M. Getz, former head of the Boston Theological Institute, first suggested that I consider Weston Jesuit School of Theology, now School of Theology and Ministry at Boston College. I am grateful for her wise suggestion. Thank you to Phyllis Blum Cole in whose Harvard Divinity School course I deduced the impact of mother loss on adult spirituality. Sister Beatrice Ste. Marie, SSND, gave me her mother's jewelry box, which became symbolic of my work.

Through a guided meditation, the Rev. R. Cameron Borton helped me discover the image of God as compassionate editor. Thank you to Brita L. Gill-Austern for asking me for a visual image of a compassionate editor in her course at Andover Newton Theological School. Joan Borton has been especially appreciative of my desire to participate in religious education through Sunday school classes of my design and more recently my book *An Artistic Approach to New Testament Literature.* My high school friend Sharon Martin Kachmar, who became a high school guidance counselor, was adjunct to divine guidance.

Thank you also to Daniel J. Harrington, SJ, for his New Testament courses and books and ongoing understanding of me as an artist and poet. J. Randall Sachs, SJ, heartened me with his understanding of why blue matters to me and our shared notice of Gerard Manley Hopkins's notations with drawing of bluebell flowers. In a course on Isaiah taught by Richard J. Clifford, SJ, my thoughts on texture (which is an artistic element that I applied to biblical passages in other courses) deepened because Isaiah is often quoted in the New Testament. I acknowledge with gratitude the other professors who taught at Weston Jesuit School of Theology when I was a student and who are mentioned in this book: Francine Cardman, James F. Keenan, SJ, John S, Kselman, SS, Roger D. Haight, SJ, Brian O. McDermott, SJ, and John O'Donnell, SJ.

Thank you to Loulla Efstathiou and Meg Herman for sharing their stories of mother loss in the essay about God as transcendent good will. Betty and John Erkkila, Ann Rogers, and Judy Rumbaoa are part of the story of the indigo buntings. Women friends who are mentioned in the last chapters of this book deserve recognition. I am cheered by my sister Rosemary Lesch and friends Jane Carr, Carol Christoffers, Sarah Clark, Barbara Hansen, Ruth Kahn, Pat LaFramboise, Jocelyn McWhirter, Robina Quale-Leach, and Gay Williams.

I am grateful to Robina Quale-Leach for her understanding of me and for her perceptive foreword. Thank you to Elizabeth Barnett, who is the literary executor for Edna St. Vincent Millay and The Edna St. Vincent Millay Society, for allowing me to include verses by Edna St. Vincent Millay in my book.

Thank you to the *Gloucester Daily* Times that first published "Other Rocks, Other Colors."

April Blessing, Freebie, and *Indigo Bunting Sonnet* were published in the *Gloucester Daily Times* and the *Record-Journal* of Meriden, Connecticut. The *Record-Journal* allowed me to republish *Chipmunks' Christmas Cabin* and *Sandy's Special Gift,* which were originally published in *Town Times.* I am thankful for publication in the weekly *Town Times* as well as in the poetry section, *Pennons of Pegasus,* of the *Record-Journal,* which is edited by Lois Lake Church. Because I wrote for these papers, my skills grew.

By writing these acknowledgments I see how the pieces of the past fit together. Gratitude that lifts my heart is blessing for me. In turn I wish happiness to all who have graced my path to publication.

Foreword

THIS IS A VERY different book from its two immediate predecessors, *An Artistic Approach to New Testament Literature* and *Portfolio of Painterly Poems*. *An Artistic Approach* presents clearly laid-out insights into the background of each book of the New Testament, each book's text, and how each book has been used since its composition. It shows how each book applies the artistic principles of line, form, color, and texture. It also gives useful suggestions for activities for Christian education programs at all age levels. *Painterly Poems* offers insightful poems and drawings, grouped intelligently under the headings of "Calling," "Continuance," and "Completion."

Those who can organize materials so well have often learned to do so because they feel an unusually strong need to make sense out of disordered experiences. This book gives you a sense of how Sharon Chace's capacity for order stems from a life that, ever since her premature birth, has been constantly and somewhat frustratingly disordered by a low level of physical coordination. All her life, she has had to be enough of an observer from the sidelines so that she has had opportunities to observe much that a more-active participant might fail to notice. She has had to look into herself, to understand her own situation, and she has had to look into the selves of others, to understand how she and they can be mutually sustaining. Insight, sight-into, has been her way of life.

It becomes apparent, as one reads this collection of essays written at various stages of Sharon's growth in faith and understanding, that her insights come to her from all directions rather than arriving in a steady, unidirectional procession. Ever since I recognized her unusual gifts as a student in the first history class she took with me at Albion College in the 1960s, she has given me the pleasure and privilege of sharing her insights with me. I am glad that you, too, now have the opportunity to come to know her better in the pages of this book.

Robina Quale-Leach
Professor Emerita of History, Albion College
June 5, 2009

Introduction

"As shoes for your feet put on whatever will make you ready to proclaim the gospel of peace."

(Eph 6:15)

Someone stole my boots and my Bible. This minor yet memorable heist happened when I was a college freshman. In 1962, I was a proper young woman who wore heels when traveling by plane between Detroit and Boston. I carried my boots and a small New Testament with my name and a picture of the First Congregational Church of Rockport, Massachusetts, glued inside the front cover, in a plaid shoe bag. One day, I left the bag on a couch in the woman's lounge and someone stole it. Because this particular New Testament had my name in it as well as the name and location of my church, I hoped that the thief would return my Bible. That did not happen.

The loss of Bible and boots was not a problem. I needed new boots anyway, and there were many Bibles in the Albion College bookstore. Yet the theft of boots and Bible is a metaphor for all the forces that derailed me along the way.

During my years at Albion College, a college in Albion, Michigan, related to the Methodist Church, I wanted to become a director of religious education. Everyone said that choice was not a good idea. People had a wide range of motivations for discouraging me, yet the reason was always the same. *You do not have the physical stamina.* Professors in the art department wondered if I had the physical strength to hold my paintbrush. Between my junior and senior year the most chilling remark about my desire to be a director of religious education came from the late Dr. Coy James, a very devout Methodist and at the time chair of the history department. "You will work very hard. No one will know how hard you worked. The work will kill you, and then they will pick the bones."

Even with my lack of physical stamina, which I have only recently learned stems from having been a premature baby in an age where not many babies of my birth weight lived to my current age, I continued to think of myself as a church worker. Still, in 1967, I gave up seminary after the first year to put my husband through his graduate studies. I begged him to take time off so I could finish, but for various reasons that was not to be. Postponement of my dreams turned out for the best. If Ernie had not been compulsive about parish work, I would not have met my friend, Doris.

Often church people have not understood my lack of stamina. My older friend, Doris, from the first parish that my United Church of Christ minister-husband and I served, gave the gift of understanding and expressed her feelings in a more gentle way than did Dr. James. "You have not received quite enough recognition. People do not understand how long it takes to do the things you do." People in both the rural New Hampshire church and a New Jersey suburban church eventually caught on, and we have gone to joyous reunions. I expect that in our retirement years and in my recent return to my hometown other Puritan punctures will heal. Meanwhile, I have sustaining memories of color and light, welcome and goodwill at St. Andrew's Episcopal Church in Meriden, Connecticut.

Sometimes God gives people a second chance. Or maybe what seems like a second chance is the first real one. My second chance came in the mid-'80s when Dr. Lorine M. Getz, who taught the course *Religion, Society, and the Arts* that I took as a special student at Andover Newton Theological School, suggested that I apply for full-time study at Weston Jesuit School of Theology. "Why would a *dyed-in-the-wool Protestant* want to do that?" I asked. "Because you need their library; it is the best in theological aesthetics," explained Dr. Getz. In time the flip side of my hermeneutic of suspicion became a hermeneutic of surprise.

My husband left the parish ministry. Sermons on graph paper were a big hint that his most natural skills are in engineering and quality control. During my graduate school career, I went with my husband on his business trip to Hershey, Pennsylvania, where he attended a meeting of replacement window engineers. Before the trip I mended his dress pants. He forgot to pack them. So we went to a store to buy more. I scrutinized the men's pant section. Ernie wandered off. Soon he came back to the men's department with a grin on his face. "Guess what I found?" he asked with glee.

You guessed it. *Shoes.* The shoe department was closing. There was a pile of size-six shoes for two dollars a pair: low heels, black flats and red flats, walking shoes, boots, and gold slippers. Not only did I buy them; I wore most of them out walking and even, on good days, running throughout Cambridge. Wearing them made me laugh, remembering that John Bunyan, who wrote *The Pilgrim's Progress,* believed in prayer and shoes as needed equipment for pilgrims in their holy skirmishes with vices and temptations. With all that walking, my feet grew larger, as did heart hopes. The intellectual and spiritual life that my Jesuit education opened for me strengthened my heart, mind, and soul.

In time the right way for me to be part of religious education opened up. Writing became my way of giving back to God and life. The earliest foreshadowing came in 1970 when I taught Sunday school in the First Congregational Church of Walpole, New Hampshire, and my children's meditation *Celebration Is* was published in *Colloquy. Pockets* magazine published my children's story *Day of the Starfish* in 1995. *When Baby Jesus Grows Up: A Children's Christmas Program,* which is a poem play, was published in 1998 by CSS Publishing. Resource Publications, which is an imprint of Wipf and Stock, published my *Portfolio of Painterly Poems: A Pilgrim's Path to God* in 2006. In 2008, Wipf and Stock published my book *An Artistic Approach to New Testament Literature,* and then the book was picked up by The Lutterworth Press for European distribution. I learned of Lutterworth's publishing plans after returning from an Albion College Homecoming and my book signing. How appropriate, since Albion is another word for England and I am of English ancestry! To take off on John Wesley, who said that the world was his parish, I am starting to feel like the world is my Sunday school.

Although my New Testament book project includes some personal experiences that intersect with academics, this book is more personal. The main question that this book addresses is: What evidence is there for the existence of God? Styles of discourse matter. In the Weston Jesuit School of Theology course *Two Great Councils: Trent and Vatican II,* Father John W. O'Malley discussed the councils in terms of styles of discourse. He also applied his rhetorical analysis to the Vatican II in his books *What Happened At Vatican II?* and *Trent and All That: Renaming Catholicism in the Early Modern Era.* Contrasting styles of discourse have been present in churches and cultures throughout the centuries. To summarize O'Malley's thought, there are four styles of discourse in western culture. Style 1 is dogmatic. Catholic classicists and Protestant fundamentalists often speak dogmatically. Style 2 is scientific. Point-by-point statements are characteristic of this style. Style 3 is literary. A literary style is most characterized by tolerance of ambiguity. Style 4 is artistic. In its purest form, an artistic style of discourse is wordless. Think dance and paintings. In addressing the existence of God, my style is literary and at times artistic.

My literary style is interconnected with my understanding of how God speaks to human hearts. My premise is that need invites revelation, and God is perceived through human sensitivities of intellect and imagination. Two very different people, Martin Luther and Emily Dickinson, inform my thought. In his book, *Here I Stand: A Life of Martin Luther*, Roland Bainton said, "Luther verged on saying that an excessive emotional sensitivity is a mode of revelation."[1] Emily Dickinson also suggested that emotional sensitivity can invite insight. She said, "Success is counted sweetest/ By those who ne'er succeed./ To comprehend a nectar/ Requires sorest need."[2]

I write about myself and my journey from dimness of soul toward clearer vision and deeper trust that God is. Yet more importantly, this book is about God and God's mysterious ways. As Francine Cardman reminded her students in her course on the history of spirituality, religious memoirs are more about God than self. Like most people, I at times have doubts, yet doubt serves me well because it guards against making exaggerated claims. As Martin E. Marty wrote, "Doubt and unfaith are the very fuel on which faith feeds."[3]

With doubt spurring on my search, the main mission statement of this book is to share moments of insight that suggest that God is. My assignment came as close as it gets to a direct word from God him or herself. My pink hiking boots are the shoes most symbolic of my task to trust and keep on writing a message of peace that God is. The following poem came out of what we called in the '60s a *happening*. In a discouraging moment on June 24 in 2002, I tried the open the Bible and point method. My fingers landed on the last verse in Haggai, which is not a favored passage to which my Bible would naturally open. The passage reads: "'On that day, says the LORD of hosts, I will take you O Zerubbabel

1. Bainton, *Here I Stand: A Life of Martin Luther*, 283.
2. Linscott, ed., *Selected Poems & Letters of Emily Dickinson*, 38.
3. Marty, "A Profile of Norman Lear: Another Pilgrim's Progress," 57.

my servant, son of Shealtiel, says the LORD, and make you like a signet ring; for I have chosen you, says the LORD of hosts'" (Hag 2:23 NRSV). Throughout the Old Testament book of Haggai, there are references to the twenty-fourth day of various months and specifically the sixth month in 1:15. The sixth month in the calendar of the time was not June but rather August or September. Still, in my reader response approach I immediately identified the sixth month with our June.

At the very least this experience is copious coincidence. While I believe this serendipitous happening is from God, complete certainty is as overconfident as a non-theistic interpretation that there is a remarkable inner concordance in my subconscious. Overstatement does not create sacred space for wonder. There is room for mystery here. In any case, my personal application of it would be unthinkable and likely a home-grown delusion from the soil of insecurity if I had not landed on it by challenging chance or divine design.

Haggai would make a good Protestant poster child for a stewardship campaign or a Catholic patron saint of fundraising for either a building fund or social action mission. Haggai's spiritual concern went beyond buildings. Yet creating a place of worship was basic to his understanding of what it means to live to the glory of God.

His people had homes but had let the house of the Lord fall into disrepair. His basic message was that their lives were not going well, so they might as well start rebuilding the temple. Trust God, take courage, and believe in God's presence. Haggai assured the older people who remembered the glory of the former temple that the new one would be even better. Renovation work started "on the twenty-fourth day of the month, in the sixth month" (Hag 1:15). Blessings started to flow back into their community after the foundation was laid and the temple cleansed and rededicated (Hag 2:1–19). Although Haggai would not use the word *empiricism*, there is a sense here that God is trustworthy because trusting in God worked. In the last verses of Haggai, God speaks through Haggai to the governor and God's servant Zerubbabel and makes him like a signet ring, which symbolizes the power to lead. Thus Haggai gave hope for the future.

For me to be chosen to be like God's jewelry suggests to me that my writings will have a part in helping people believe in work and trust that God is. People who work and rely on God's presence build up churches, yet trust in God is more universal than a particular temple or church. Like Zerubbabel, people may with courage work and trust long before consciously choosing to be God's jewelry. The story of rebuilding the temple continues in Ezra and Zechariah. Zechariah says that Zerubbabel laid the foundations of the new temple and his hands will complete it (Zech 4:9–10). Whether one is entirely convinced that there is a God, building caring communities and living as if God exists are ongoing signs of love that are fueled by work and trust. Many other people will be signs, and far better signs than am I, that God is.

Maybe God has a sense of humor. My Aunt Betty died during my last year at Weston when I lived two days a week with the nuns at St. John's Residence. I inherited her jewelry; enough pearls to keep me proper in the most formal Episcopal churches, should we ever permanently go that route. Sister Bea was hanging on to a large jewelry box that had belonged to her mother until she found the right person for it. Of course, that person was me, and in time the directive to be metaphorically God's jewelry would be funny and fitting.

Love's Jewelry

God charged me with a calling
that is not for me alone.
Current-like strength surged
through me on June 24, 2002
and my fingers rested on
the biblical words . . .
And make you like a signet ring;
For I have chosen you, says the
Lord of hosts (Hag 2:23).
Those words came through prophet
Haggai on the twenty-fourth day
of the month to Zerubbabel.
His task was to help his people
believe that God was with them
and rebuilding the temple to
honor God was a holy task.
Even before his grant of
authority to act on God's behalf
symbolized by a signet ring
Zerubbabel practiced
courage, trust, hope, and
work to God's glory.
Anyone with desire can aspire
to be God's jewelry by taking

courage and striving to honor
God even in the littlest and often
quiet, invisible ways of trying,
trusting, caring, and sharing.
For not all work, like not all
jewelry, is splashy.
Polishing perfects gems, be they
diamonds or humble tiger's-eye.
Practice invites peace and presence
into hearts of known and unknown
friends of God.
From inner facets of faith, people
grow and glow as shining signs that
God is and will be forever more.

This book is for all, whether lifelong believers or skeptics or seekers who yearn for God. People need food and water. Although they are not distributed fairly, these things exist. Some of us know that we need God. Need may be the first hint that God is. Glimpses of God in this book are presented as neither dogma nor science but as reflections in poetry, prose, and prayer.

Part 1

Sincerely Sharon

1

A Theological Problem

I have had a number of experiences that are as close as it gets to divine intervention. Even entertaining the idea of divine help presents theological problems. The main question is why would God give me clear directions and even intervene in my personal life when other people are washed away in torrents of water or floods of tears?

The best answer that I can offer came from an unexpected source. In 2008, about thirty years after I first read it, I reread *The Language of the Gospel: Early Christian Rhetoric* by Amos N. Wilder. Writing about New Testament narratives of miraculous healings and deliverances, he said that such intervention could be seen not as isolated cases "but as a manifestation of a general redemption for the whole people of God."[1] Therefore I believe that my personal stories about surprising guidance and assistance suggest that there can be transcendent help, whether through divine or human good will. A logical and heartfelt conclusion is that ultimately justice will prevail.

I shared my findings with Dr. Martin E. Marty who, before his retirement, was the Fairfax M. Cone Distinguished Professor of the History of Modern Christianity at the University of Chicago, as well as senior editor of *The Christian Century*. He continues to be an authoritative writer on religion and interpreter of the religious landscape. He answered, "With Amos Wilder and you I like to think of 'manifestations of a general redemption for the whole people of God,' which we are free to render specific as redemption to each of us, as we go and come—in your case to Rockport, and to new adventures."

1. Wilder, *The Language Of the Gospel*, 71.

Yes indeed, our return to Rockport has redemptive features, as you will see in following chapters. My Weston Jesuit education was also part of salvaging my best life. Times of trouble have been redeemed or exchanged into good things like the green saving stamps of the 1950s that could be redeemed for products that householders needed. The message from my experiences may be that there is indeed personal love in the heart of the universe. My readers will have their own thoughts, questions, and conclusions.

2

Protestant Pulse

Turnings of My Heart

When people learned that I, a middle-aged mother and wife of a husband who had been a United Church of Christ minister for ten years, was studying at Weston Jesuit School of Theology, they had one basic question. Most people felt that it was not polite to voice their main concern, but a few less-reticent folk asked directly, "Are you going to turn Catholic?"

The answer to that question was, and remains, no. Yet I have become a different kind of Protestant. On Valentine's Day 1995 I wore a heart monitor to school. My classmates were horrified and said, "Don't run—that thing makes us nervous!" I said, "Don't worry. I am just documenting the Protestant pulse!" My journal recorded my spiritual pulse and the turnings of my heart.

My heart beats slowly. I have a crock-pot personality and am slow to warm up. Stewing brings out my best ideas. At an Albion College reunion over twenty-five years ago, my favorite English teacher, Elsie Munro, suggested that instead of piling on classes at the Protestant seminary where I was a special student, I might better take time off to think about my courses. She was premature but had a point. Since my graduation from Weston Jesuit, I continue to reflect. Following advice from Fr. Daniel J. Harrington, SJ, that dovetails with Miss Munro's suggestions, I keep on doing the things I do reasonably well—writing and art. If my art goes awry, I turn to baking. My cookies flavored with "demon rum" have been eaten at *The Christian Century*, which is a biweekly journal featuring articles about religion in the news, book reviews, and theological essays.

I first met my friend Dr. Lorine M. Getz when I was her student. She immediately saw beyond my fragility and fatigue, my clumsiness and "creative spelling," to the conscientious student that I am. When the time was right for me to consider a degree program, she suggested Weston. "Why?" I asked. "You need their library," she replied. Yes, I needed books and more. Following are personal highlights of my journey from a loss of inner sight to a happier Sharon with deeper delight in grace.

On visiting day at Weston Jesuit School of Theology I came to the point and said, "A lot of emphasis is rightly put on service to the church. As a pastor's wife, I was about as good at strenuous service as St. Therese of Lisieux was at being an energetic nun! I like to curl up in an afghan and read." Fr. Brian O. McDermott, SJ, who at the time was academic dean, replied, "You would be welcome here."

Ignatius of Loyola was the founder of the Society of Jesus (also known as the Jesuits). Along with rigorous courses in theology, biblical studies, ethics, and church history, most students at Weston take a course in Ignatian studies. I confessed that Ignatian studies were of interest to me because I had read *Ignatius of Loyola: The Psychology of a Saint* by W. W. Meissner, SJ, MD. As a young boy, St. Ignatius lost his mother. My manuscript in circulation was about the adult religious lives of women who as young girls had lost their mothers through death as I, too, had. Fr. McDermott said that he did not know what the coincidence meant but that he was reading Meissner's book and had just gotten to the point where St. Ignatius's mother died.

I applied to Weston Jesuit School of Theology knowing that my basic goal was to further the best use of my life, but I lacked certainty about how to use my gifts vocationally. My central spiritual dilemma was clear. As would often be my practice at Weston, I silently quoted to myself a hymn from the *Pilgrim Hymnal*. The last words from the second verse of *Spirit of God Descend upon My Heart* summarized my condition. "But take the dimness of my soul away."[1] Clarity in one's personal life makes it easier to see God.

Students usually conclude their studies at Weston with a course in Ignatian spirituality. I started with Fr. McDermott's course, "The

1. "Spirit of God, Descend upon My Heart," *Pilgrim Hymnal*, 232.

Theological and Pastoral Dimensions of the Spiritual Exercises of St. Ignatius of Loyola." My heart warmed. Faith rekindled. I identified a need to find peace between my warring verbal and artistic sides. Fr. McDermott implied, I believe, a need for a more relational theology and a deeper understanding of God as personal. He wrote on one of my papers that the organic model can be affirmed, but it needs to be critiqued by John Macmurray and the form of the personal model because the organic model has limits that the personal model overcomes. Of course, I wrote my paper out of an organic or natural theology. After all, in college I read Tillich, Whitehead, and at least in secondary sources Hartshorne, as well as Emerson and Thoreau. While I have always been certain that God is in an earthly creative process, I have always been a little iffy about whether God is ultimately personal and that there is a resurrected life that is more personal than an oceanic fusion.

Although I did not check into John Macmurray immediately nor did I ask Professor McDermott more specifically what he thought I needed to learn, we both in the long run had our way. While I also found God in nature and art, during the Ignatian course I discovered a more personal God by writing as a self-assigned project a children's story, *Chipmunk's Christmas Cabin*. By writing this story I more deeply affirmed my growing conviction that direction from a personal God can come when people quietly pray and seek discernment. Through imaginative participation in St. Ignatius's masterpiece *The Spiritual Exercises*, his followers grow in relationship to Christ and discern their callings. My self-assigned writing extended the discernment process of discovering God's caring beyond the Ignatian course, which included a modified experience of *The Spiritual Exercises*.

Certainly I was writing in a contemplative way and feeling my way beyond thought. In retrospect, was I also without knowing it writing as an agent in an action that would bring felt knowledge in the manner that John Macmurray describes? I do not know, but I entertain the possibility that in writing I came to a deeper understanding of God. Macmurray wrote, "The reflective moment in a practical activity is itself concerned with the means to the realization of a practical end; and in many cases the knowledge it achieves can be applied in different activities than the one for which it was originally intended."[2] It was not my paper with a grade of A- that Fr. McDermott asked to keep. He wanted a copy of my chipmunk

2. Macmurray, *The Self as Agent*, 182.

story. In the decade after graduation, I wrote more stories that evoked latent beliefs.

It is hard to say exactly when my art and writing synthesized in poetry, but certainly the process sped up through my participation in poetry readings by Weston Jesuit and Episcopal Divinity School students. Feelings and hearts aflame or stilled by awe are present prior to poetry. During my very first semester, thanks to Saint Ignatius of Loyola, sustaining foundational experiences rose through accumulated debris in memory. I imagine both St. Ignatius and John Wesley smiling. The Rev. and Mrs. Jonathan Edwards, who are my spiritual ancestors, would be pleased also. Hearts on fire unite spiritual friends of different centuries and cultures. During my graduate days and afterward my heart turned toward deepening trust in God, and I found ways to imagine God.

In the course we experienced a modified version of St. Ignatius' *Spiritual Exercises.* A door into the process for all participants is a prayer to Jesus on the cross. I balked. My hesitation did not stem from my liberal Protestant bias that emphasizes God more than Jesus. I hesitated because I had been hurt by sarcasm because of my faith in Jesus and crushed in his name by unfair critique of my understandings of salvation. Relatives did not understand my interest in religion. Yet I made my own decisions. Their disinterest turned into ridicule. Nature pushed. Grace pulled. I had an art major and English and religion minors at Albion College.

In time, my husband's sermons written on graph paper yielded to more appropriate work as a quality control manager and engineer. His theology is less orthodox than is mine. However, as a young seminarian, he was sanctimoniously squared in his belief that my Christology was inadequate. In the Ignatian course, I was not going anywhere without praying. Prayer brought the realization that I crucify Christ by not truly believing that Christ cares for people like me who have limitations. It was time to reclaim a foundational experience. At the age of eight I noticed that the pastor of the evangelical Sunday school and the Sunday school teacher at the Universalist Church I attended when we lived in another section of town were very different, but both taught that God loves all people equally. That was indeed good news for me, the clumsy one on the playground and at home. Imagination, a bridge to truth, released an inkling of the risen Christ. Jesus was not pleased with my husband's attitude. Yet I saw that a compassionate Jesus understood the division in his soul. A favorite gospel hymn came to mind: "What a Friend We Have in Jesus."

My heart opened to welcome guidance through more prayer dialogue. In the most non-Protestant moment of my life, I prayed to St. Ignatius of Loyola while looking at his picture.

"So what do you notice?" I imagined St. Ignatius asking me that question. The dialogue that follows is imaginary yet felt very real and perhaps is in a spiritual dimension that is not provable.

"My desk is narrow and brown like yours."

"What else?"

"I've never noticed the crucifix before over your desk."

"What about it?"

"The modeling in dark and light and the same light that is illuminating Christ is shining on you."

"What is over your desk?"

"My shadow box with the sand dollar."

"So?"

"That's my legendary and natural symbol of Christ."

"So you are not doing your writing for me but for Christ."

"Yes."

"Just keep going.'" I did, and during the course and the following summer I wrote five children's stories as my way of more deeply internalizing *The Spiritual Exercises.*

When you give a Protestant like me a mission, it is a good thing St. Ignatius has a whole company of helpers here below. Someone asked how the course, "Two Great Councils: Trent and Vatican II," was going. "Really keeping the Protestant work ethic alive," I replied. I delved into writing my paper comparing the treatment of Vatican II by *The Christian Century* and *Commonweal.*

"Remember, it is just a paper," said Professor John W. O'Malley, SJ. I felt loved by God through Fr. O'Malley's words. I defend "justification by faith alone" but lack heartfelt conviction. Release from pressure made it possible for me to write a paper worthy of sharing with my elderly friend, Doris. My trust deepened, and my identity as a Christian widened. Professor O'Malley's method of comparing councils by style of discourse referred to in the introduction to this book helped me understand that my religious orientation transcends ecclesiastical boundaries.

My concentration in biblical studies brought continuity and change. Professor Emeritus of Old Testament at Boston University School of Theology, Dr. Harrell F. Beck, spoke to the women's fellowship at a

Congregational church shortly before he died. I asked what to his mind had been the most exciting developments in biblical scholarship in the last ten years. He said, "The rise in Catholic scholarship." *Bingo.* Students at Weston can feel the excitement. No wonder Weston, now the School of Theology and Ministry at Boston College, is the home of *New Testament Abstracts.*

Like my Methodist religion professors at Albion College, professors at Weston stress the integration of faith and knowledge. This shared concern gave me continuity, as did the ongoing concern for historical criticism. There are new developments. Today just about any field can be a lens through which to examine biblical texts. There are literary, sociological, psychological, and reader-response approaches to biblical studies.

As an artist I started to look at the Bible from artistic angles. During an Old Testament course taught by Fr. John S, Kselman, SS, I first considered the role of the colors blue, green, and red in the Bible and discovered how my first experience of God is tied to biblical texts. When I was three and a half my mother was dying of leukemia. Soothing light filtered through cobalt blue vases. Blue was grace and a sight of God's face as it was for the Hebrew elders in Exodus 24 that records their climb up a mountain where they saw the face of God with a pavement of sapphire stones under God's feet. I painted an abstract and wrote a poem based on that passage. Blue splotches suggest the sapphire pavement and a red freeform dot is a symbol for God's footprint. In time I wrote the chapter in this book, "Envisioning God through Biblical Color Images."

Color is one of the formal art elements. The others are line, form, and texture. In a personal fullness of time I applied those formal art elements to biblical literature and wrote my book, *An Artistic Approach to New Testament Literature.* Describing biblical texts according to the formal art elements started when I took the course "Mark," which was taught by Fr. Daniel J. Harrington, SJ. He said that we could address our papers to someone other than himself. Of course, we would write with a sense of him reading over our shoulders. I wrote my paper to my daughter, Amy, who at the time was a student with a psychology major and art minor at Keene State College in Keene, New Hampshire. I described the feeding of the five thousand that is recorded in Mark 6:34–44 according to color, texture, line, and form. Color is an actual color, green. Mark was the only evangelist to tell us the color of the grass. Texture is the allusion by the color green to the green pastures of Psalm 23. The form is the type of writing. In this case the form was a story and line was the plot line. Other artistic characteristics that I have used to explore other biblical passages are perspective, balance, and contrast in dark and light.

During my graduate school days an unexpected move to Connecticut opened my eyes to other faith communities and vistas of artistic beauty. I still value clear glass Congregational church windows that symbolize openness to other steeples. We lived in Rockport, Massachusetts, and Ernie worked in Peabody for a window manufacturer as an engineer and quality control manager. Although the following poem is about a relative who was not a church person, it also expresses the feelings of some church women who were so mad that they did not have the minister's wife of their dreams that they saw me as a second minister's wife and felt they could say anything they wanted to me. In time I did return, but Memorial Day 1995 was a turning point.

Memorial Day, 1995

"I will say to you
anything I want,
anytime I want,
in any way I want."
Stinging rays, spoken
in perfect grammar,
syntax, and diction,
stunned but did
not kill me.
"No, you won't,"
I replied.
Claiming my freedom
I walked out—
never to return.

I told Dean McDermott that I could not stand Rockport much longer, but because Ernie did not want to leave, I did not want to move unless the decision was clear. A few days later he lost his job and received a better one in Connecticut the next day. "Close as it gets to divine intervention," I said to Professor Harrington, who replied, "Yes, I know. Congratulations." At the time I commuted to Cambridge by train and subway. My train friends were of one voice, "You are so lucky. You are being guided all the way. Most of us have to muddle along the best we can."

The day before we moved there was a full-circle rainbow over Sandy Bay, which brought forth hope. This miraculous move to Connecticut strengthened my academic life and deepened my sense of belonging. I went to Yale for a semester, which, of course, was broadening. When Professors Leander E. Keck and Christopher R. Seitz learned that at Weston Jesuit I painted a picture of God based on Exodus 24:9–10, they promptly asked me to paint a picture of God based on Exodus 33:17–23. I did an abstract that suggests God's glory in pinks, yellows, and oranges and presence suggested by shadow. When God's face is hidden, God may be seen in shadows and signs. As much as I loved Yale I felt homesick for Weston and the consolation of feeling part of a spiritual family even as metaphorically speaking a distant Protestant cousin. I prayed to St. Ignatius and imagined him saying, "Of course I have no problems with Yale. Who published the book you are holding? But the question is, 'Which school has the sunshine?'"

In order for me to finish up my degree work at Weston, Ernie drove me to school during the last three semesters, when I stayed two days a week with sisters who were on Sabbatical. Sisters and Sharon! Welcome and acceptance were signs that God is. Except for the crucifix on my bedroom wall and occasional wine with dinner, life was like my college life in Susanna Wesley Hall. Sharing stories, eating together, and a discussion led by Dean McDermott on centering prayer that was not tied to a Puritan agenda, "Learn to meditate and you can drive," were stimulating and also soothing to my sometimes-shaken self.

The defining moments of my callings came through professors' comments, direct questions, dreams, and the focus of fatigue. Professor Roger D. Haight, SJ, kept my poem "The Mind of God" and said that maybe I had found my medium. Yes, I also found my voice. There were darkly printed words in my childhood memory: "I don't know if you could write poetry. You do not have enough rhythm." Fear of failure faded. Fr. John O'Donnell, SJ, asked what we wanted to do. "Develop and teach biblical literature from aesthetic perspectives," was my response. His affirming nod meant a great deal.

In addition to clarity of purpose that came by answering a question, the last word in a dream was so strong it felt as if it came from outside. "Art." I started to see my life as an artistic project with the Holy Spirit as Artistic Director. This image that came to me when writing poetry as a self-assigned project while taking "Prayer in the Bible," taught by John S. Kselman, SS, allows for dialogue and questioning the Almighty.

Stance of Choice

Is screaming at God
or silent submission
the stance of choice?
If relationship with God
is a creative project,
a life-long love,
with the Holy Spirit
as Artistic Director,
then form follows function
as surely as yearnings
yield to lament and
contrition is enfolded
in waves of warmth
winding upward within.

Restoring relationships,
life made whole and hallowed,
is the function.
Form must be amoeboid.
Covenant built on repression
of grief and complaint is not
sacred bond with fellow
beings or with God.
Protest must carry the pain.
Yet sometimes, "I am sorry"
are the only words worth
uttering while standing in
dark mysteries of suffering
and sin with inner eyes open
to receive the "morning star
that rises in your hearts."

Like Professor Harrington, I do New Testament abstracts, only mine are painterly! Even in college my artistic nature and verbal side waged holy war. Considering aesthetic aspects of biblical literature unites the pieces. My poetry is painting with words. Visual images and words lay down together like the biblical lion and lamb.

Art started to be part of my worship along with the beauty of honed words in *The Book of Common Prayer.* Now in addition to the simplicity of a plain Congregational meeting house, I also love stained glass windows, especially those in St Andrew's Episcopal Church in Meriden, Connecticut. Meriden, where we lived for ten years before our second return to Rockport in 2007 when Ernie retired, is a city of hills and churches. I have painted the trap rock hills and found texture in the churches of Meriden. No longer just one brand, my faith now resonates with Wesleyan warmth, memorized Congregational hymns, and historic sermons from St. Chrysostom in an Episcopal Church. Synthesis need not be suspect.

When my heart slowed dramatically I was given the gift of focus and wrote *When Baby Jesus Grows Up: A Children's Christmas Program* and drew floral designs that now translate into glass engravings. One day I surprised myself by saying to God, "All I want to do is be a good mother and teach Sunday school." Then I added, "Am I for real or am I saying what I think you want me to say?" My sense of God's reply was, "You are telling the truth but are just not speaking literally. And you have no business teaching Sunday school right now." When talking with Fr. Daniel J. Harrington, I again surprised myself by saying, "I may do something for religious education without ever stepping foot in a classroom." He nodded.

In conclusion, I learned one meaning of my mention of mother loss on visiting day that converged with Fr. McDermott's reading about St. Ignatius's loss of his mother. My dimness was failure to believe that there is maternal love in God's heart. I embraced the gift of reflection by Fr. James F. Keenan, SJ, on Thomas Aquinas, who saw charity as the mother of the virtues. Drawing out the implications of love that gives hope, Keenan wrote in his article, "Charity, the Mother of the Virtues," "Charity is like a mother, guiding us lovingly but firmly to pursue what we love."[3] As Lutheran bumper stickers remind us, "Grace happens."

God was at work through dedicated professors, books, soul sisters, poetry readings, liturgy, and even my imagination to help me do the work I love. Writing, painting, and engraving beckon at daybreak. Play and prayer converge in the collage that is my life.

3. Keenan, "Charity, the Mother of the Virtues," 42.

3

Divine Guidance

A FOUNDATIONAL DREAM

DREAMS HAVE GUIDED ME. I have mentioned the brief dream that ended in the powerful directive, "Art." The next most significant dream I had was God's gift of guidance in 1981. In this dream I was outside in the community helping with the Brownies or Sunday school. I was agitated and hassled because my tasks were too much. I walked through our front door. Immediately a great peace came over me. God was there, and God's presence was identifiable by feeling. Then I calmly and with satisfaction found myself cutting up Swiss cheese for Ernie's lunches.

God said to me, "I hope you get to see my face." I woke up and thought "Swiss cheese—with holes—holy. I make bad puns in my sleep!" In retrospect I consider this dream to be a foundational insight because while I benefit greatly from Cape Ann programs and excursions to different places, my work is mainly done at home.

HAPPENINGS

Approximately thirty times when feeling close to desperate, I opened the Bible, ran my finger down the page, and landed on a passage of guidance. While this approach goes against my usual thinking, it worked. All the biblical passages met the platinum standard for compassion. If you try this, please let your interpretation be guided by charity.

This phenomenon or happening could be understood as inner editing or having a subconscious, inner concordance that directed me to just the words I needed to evoke my own best thoughts or beliefs. I think that the explanation of inner concordance puts too much emphasis on subconscious intelligence and on me. On the other hand, to definitely say it was God guiding me is overly confident. In either case there is an external dimension either from a state of mind that is outside of the usual state of consciousness or from a transcendent force or being. I believe it is best to say that while I feel the guidance is from God and is, therefore, a big hint that God is, there is mystery in how I landed on the right empowering verses.

Rather than presenting the most important happenings in chronological order, I have grouped them into categories. These divisions are greetings and affirmation, ethics, work, presence and help, and beauty.

Greetings and Affirmation

While I have listed and numbered the happenings inside the front and back covers of my copy of *The New English Bible: The New Testament,* I did not at first date them. Thus I have to approximate the dates of the first several happenings. I used several different versions of the Bible but quote in this essay from the New Revised Standard Version. The very first experience of finding the right verse came in the 1980s when I opened to 2 Thessalonians 1:2: "Grace to you and peace from God our Father and the Lord Jesus Christ." I felt personally greeted.

Personal affirmations are related to personal greetings. The importance of accepting my limitations while believing that there is strength for the journey is the message that 1 Corinthians 10:13 evoked sometime in the 1980s: "No testing has overtaken you that is not common to everyone. God is faithful, and he will not let you be tested beyond your strength, but with the testing he will also provide the way out so that you may be able to endure it." On September 7, 1999, I experienced my impromptu reading of Luke 21:1–4 as God telling me that I am doing a lot with my widow's mite of energy. "He looked up and saw rich people putting their gifts into the treasury; he also saw a poor widow put in two small copper coins. He said, 'Truly I tell you, this poor widow has put in more than all of them; for all of them have contributed out of their abundance, but she out of her poverty has put in all she had to live on.'"

Ethics

In short, ethical guidance to me is to do away with malice, be courageous, and trust. "Rid yourselves, therefore of all malice, and all guile, insincerity, envy and all slander" (1 Pet 2:1). I have never slandered but have followed temptation to use words to curse rather than bless. I admire the stance of the late John Deedy, writer and commentator on all things Catholic and former managing editor of *Commonweal.* He said in personal conversation to never be harder than need be.

"Be strong, and let your heart take courage, all you who wait for the LORD" (Ps 31:24). Yes, in one word *courage.* Finally, trust that supports courage is the most basic attitude of faith in life and in God. While the theme of trust in God is woven throughout the Bible, my personalized instruction to trust in myself came from verses that some ancient authorities add to chapter 26 in the apocryphal book Sirach. The verses I landed on imply that God also wants me to trust or believe in myself. "Seek a fertile field within the whole plain, and sow it with your own seed, trusting in your fine stock" (Sir 26:20).

Work

The work assignment that came to me from Haggai on June 24, 2002, is most explicit. Yet two consecutive happenings probably about a year apart in the 1980s suggested to me the first time that I must persist and work without limit because in God labor cannot be lost. Persistence, which is one of Luke's themes (1 Cor 15:58), seemed directly applicable to me when, on the second happening, I landed on Luke 18:1–8. Rather than quoting the whole passage, I will summarize the story. A widow pestered an unjust judge and wore him out with her persistence, and he did right by her. Luke's conviction is that God will vindicate his chosen.

During my last semester in 1998 at Weston I was worried that something might interfere with my schooling. God is not a red dot, but a red dot is a symbol for God in in the painting of Exodus 24:9–10 that I discuss in the chapter "Protestant Pulse: Turnings of My Heart" and the chapter "Envisioning God through Biblical Color Images." One day I uncharacteristically left an open Bible on the floor while I was painting an abstract. The next day I noticed a red blob of paint like the red dot on my Exodus painting. The verse that the paint landed on is Revelation 3:8. "I know your works. Look, I have set before you an open door, which no one is able to shut. I know that you have but little power, and yet you have kept my word and have not denied my name." Those words have comforted and sustained me. When rejection letters came before acceptance letters, I claimed the promise of open doors that no one can shut. And yes, I had little or no power, especially as a young person when my faith, although liberal and bridge-building, was met with derision.

Presence and Help

Since I have a history of almost falling through the cracks, a Bible verse that is the basis of comforting benedictions in many churches offered me assurance of support. Probably in the early 1990s Jude 1:24 gave me a blessing: "Now to him who is able to keep you from falling . . ."

On April 27, 2005, I received a message of help: "I will help you, says the LORD; your Redeemer is the Holy One of Israel" (Isa 41:14). Then in November 2005, Psalm 68:12–13 spoke to me. "'The kings of the armies, they flee, they flee!' The women at home divide the spoil, though they stay among the sheepfolds—the wings of a dove covered with silver, its pinions with green gold." In the original context this verse is enigmatic. Yet my reader response was that my friend also named Sharon and I were the women at home who would eventually reap the rewards of the battle, like the struggles of writing. At the time I worked at home on my poetry book project and my friend since high school, Sharon Martin Kachmar, who also at that time was a stay-at-home homemaker, read my manuscript and offered encouragement.

Beauty

The theme of beauty has popped up so often that I believe that my life is about theological aesthetics, and I must contemplate the significance of beauty as revelatory. In 1996 I felt it was important for me to consider beauty as a biblical concept after pondering Esther 1:11–12 when the plan was hatched for Queen Vashti to show her beauty to officials, which she refused to do. Yet her context is not mine. The directive to think about beauty remains intact. During the spring of 1999 a passage from Sirach encouraged me to continue to believe in biblical understandings of beauty. "The glory of the stars is the beauty of heaven, a glittering array in the heights of the Lord" (Sir 43:9). Beautify was the imperative in March 2001. "Beautify your face!" (2 Esd 15:54). No, I do not think that this is about not forgetting to put on a little blush so that people are not scared by my natural anemic complexion. My sense is that I should strive to make my thoughts about beauty known. Also, there is a command to make life beautiful whether experienced in the arts or in the beautiful living of love and service.

Finally, another apocryphal book, Wisdom of Solomon, depicts God as the author of beauty. In the context of dismissing natural elements such as fire, wind, and water as God, that author asserts that the Lord is better.

> For all people who were ignorant of God were foolish by nature; and they were unable from the good things that are seen to know the one who exists, nor did they recognize the artisan while paying heed to his works; but they supposed that either fire or wind or swift air, or the circle of the stars, or turbulent water, or the luminaries of heaven were the gods that rule the world. If through delight in beauty of these things people assumed them to be gods, let them know how much better than these is the Lord, for the author of beauty created them. And if people were amazed at their power and working, let them perceive from them how much more powerful is the one who formed them. For from the greatness and beauty of created things comes a corresponding perception of their Creator" (Wis 13:1–5).

While stressing the foolishness of nature worship, there is in the concluding verse 5 a sense of the "well-known Stoic argument (already used by Plato and Aristotle and repeated by Philo): we form the concept of divinity from our awareness of the world's beauty, since no beautiful thing happens by chance but is the product of creative art."[1] I must keep on with my art and writing as a way of giving back to God, who is the author of beauty.

1. Meeks, *Harper Collins Study Bible*, 1, 518.

4

Earthly Unbinding

Whenever there are earthly experiences that unbind people who are mired in shame and guilt, the freeing can be interpreted as a sign that God is. At age sixty-three I finally understood why I lack physical stamina and coordination. During a routine gynecological exam, I mentioned to my new gynecologist, Dr. Maura F. McGrane, that Ellie, who brought me up from the age of four after my mother died from leukemia, had a close to deathbed confession. She told me that when she took me in, she was told that my physical development would be very slow, and perhaps she should have listened. I simply nodded my yes. If I had been told as a young person that my poor coordination was a result of being an incubator baby and that clumsiness is inconvenient but not moral failure, I might not have been imprisoned for so many years in a shroud of shame. In the '40s, '50s, and '60s, many people still remember how President Franklin D. Roosevelt hid his polio and concluded that any limitation is something really bad. Relatives talked about me as if I did not have ears.

I told Dr. McGrane that I do not drive and that around 1970 the professor of a Keene State College graduate course, "Educating Children with Learning Disabilities," said that there are people my age who were incubator babies in small hospitals and as a result of too much oxygen have minor things wrong with their hearts, eyes, and brains. I have eye and overall coordination problems and a heart murmur and go limp after exercise. In addition to making my own pace, a pacemaker may someday be necessary for me. While various professionals have dismissed my questions, I have wondered if having been an incubator baby at about four pounds caused developmental problems.

Dr. McGrane told me that premature birth means lifelong problems and twenty years ago people did not know the long-term effects because not that many incubator babies lived a long life. She nailed the main implication: "Not serious enough to be a real disability, but no one will choose you to be on their basketball team." So true. I had sad recesses watching the other elementary school children play kickball. My leg kicked at the ball way after it was in the catcher's hands. No one wanted me on her team. Yet my classmates tried to figure out how I could play and not have my outs count, but we could not figure out how to adapt the game. Forced to play field hockey in high school on the premise that it would improve my coordination, I experienced the full meaning of "out in left field." In the driving education class, learning all the parts of the internal combustion engine was easy compared to driving with a standard transmission. I never mastered the clutch, so I was not allowed to take the driving test.

After college I did get my driver's license using an automatic transmission, but I was never comfortable driving. After eye therapy in the 1980s I did drive a little. However, practice does not always make perfect. Cars have automatic transmissions. My body does not. I never improved beyond *student driver*. It was far better to use my limited strength for graduate work at Weston Jesuit School of Theology, where I was a middle-aged Protestant wildcard, than to drive poorly to the grocery store in an effort to be "as normal as possible." Finding my voice in lively papers was freeing. The more paced pilgrimage toward the best use of my life brought out my best gifts.

About thirty years before, a college swimming class at Albion College was so hard it took away from other courses. Other students who used the kickboard to swim across the pool in the required time would get faster with practice. I just kept getting slower. Women in the health center did not know what to do when I came in limp and dizzy because they knew that graduation could be held up if the swimming course was incomplete. That semester I had an A in a New Testament course. I told the professor that I learned more about God in my swimming class because the support of my friends reflected God's love. Dr. John L. Cheek appreciated my remark.

My hometown doctor said that he did not want to get me out of swimming class because I was so conscientious that I would feel guilty for the rest of my life. Ellie said in her end-of-life conversation that she told my doctor that the swimming class was way beyond me. At last her acknowledgment of my difficulty started the final stages of my unbinding.

My emotional burden drifted even further away when my understanding gynecologist went on to make the explicit connection between being an incubator baby and adult difficulty in driving. Because of a premature baby in her family who as an adult does not drive, she knows how important it is to respect adult decisions. In my experience, there has been too little respect for my choices. My secular Puritan family did not find church appealing but I did and was very loyal until there was too much pressure. Many people concluded that my decision not to drive meant a lack of faith or psychological problems.

Storm clouds of criticism blew up suddenly and darkened my mood. My late friend Pat understood. While I was shopping once with Pat and her friend, her friend said that she would make me drive or we would not get home. Pat defended me. Now insight fashions internal windshield wipers that sweep away tears. Release from shame is a catalytic converter that decomposes hurtful memories and refreshes my writing life.

ADDENDUM

Just before sending my manuscript to the copy editor, my church's newsletter came with a surprising announcement. There will be a fun night with the movie *Mamma Mia,* and if anyone needs a ride, someone will give them one! Life changes, and so do people and attitudes. The outreach of the hospitality committee is evidence of good will in community.

Part 2

Images of God

5

God as Just Judge and Poet-Prophet

A DERIVATIVE BIBLICAL IMAGE of God as a just Judge and Poet-Prophet suggests that God interacts with people and is responsive to their requests. Because conversation is basic to being human, biblical testimony to God's willingness to engage in discussion can be interpreted as a promise that God is personal. To sum up: 1.The image and mixed metaphor of God as a just Judge and a Poet-Prophet that first appears in the Bible in Genesis 15:1–4 is supported in poetic and prose prayer embedded in biblical narrative throughout the Bible. 2. If the Bible is understood as divinely inspired, the poetry in the Bible suggests God must be a poet. 3. The most-convincing evidence for God's poetic nature is that embedded prayer reveals a prayer process, which is poetic and interactive. 4. God is ultimately beyond all metaphors.

The double metaphor of just Judge and Poet-Prophet is suggested in Genesis 15:1–6:

> After these things the word of the LORD came to Abram in a vision,"Do not be afraid, Abram, I am your shield; your reward shall be very great." But Abram said, "O Lord GOD, what will you give me, for I continue childless, and the heir of my house is Eliezer of Damascus?" And Abram said, "You have given me no offspring, and so a slave born in my house is to be my heir." But the word of the LORD came to him, "This man shall not be your heir; no one but your very own issue should be your heir." He brought him outside and said, "Look toward heaven and count the stars, if you are able to count them." Then he said to him, "So shall your descendants be." And he believed the LORD; and the LORD reckoned it to him as righteousness.

These verses show multiple dimensions of God as just Judge and Poet-Prophet. As Judge, God assesses Abram and justly reckons his faith as righteousness. As poet reassuring Abram about his prophetic mission to procreate, God speaks in a poet's voice, using words metaphorically. He says to Abram, "I am your shield." The stars in the sky poetically symbolize the many descendants that will come from Abram.

God as a just Judge and ruler is a basic and predominating emphasis in Genesis. Charged with the responsibilities of instructing the people of Israel in the ways of righteousness and justice (Gen 18:19), Abram, now Abraham, similarly dares to hold God, who might sweep away the righteous with the wicked, to the same requirements. "Shall not the Judge of all the earth do what is just?" (Gen 18:25).[1]

In my sense of things, this image of Judge is softened and enlarged by pictures of God having a poet's heart that can embrace ambiguity and engage in dialogue through a prophet's voice. As we have seen in Genesis 15:1, the word of the Lord came to Abram in a vision, assuring Abram, "I am your shield." Again in verse 4 the *word of the Lord* instructs. Word and image of the shield merge a prophet's voice with a poet's metaphor. God must have a poet's heart because God reached out in both a poetic image and also through a vision from the subconscious region that poets tap. By listening to Abraham's pleas, God proves his ability to deal with ambiguity. He can be persuaded. In the sketch of God in Genesis 18, God is not a fundamentalist, either religious or secular, who sees truth and justice only in black-and-white terms. The ability to deal with ambiguity is a characteristic of good poets, said Martin E. Marty at a conference at Episcopal Divinity School in May 1995 in response to my question, "Are there any fundamentalists who are good poets?"

There is some evidence that the talent to learn from ambiguity was valued in the ancient world. Being comfortable with the complexities of parables is a characteristic of scribes, as described in the book of Sirach, which is one of the seven books in the Apocrypha. In Sirach's view, the scribe is discerning: "He seeks out the hidden meanings of proverbs and is at home with the obscurities of parables" (Sir 39:3). Since Jesus had a prophetic voice and also spoke in parables, I deduce that the historical Jesus reflects God's attributes of Poet-Prophet.

The Bible is partly written in poetry. Poetic structure is most evident in Psalms, Proverbs, and Song of Solomon. Amos N. Wilder noted that

1. Balentine, *Prayer in the Hebrew Bible*, 196.

the Old Testament books most quoted in the New Testament are books of poetry, Isaiah and the Psalms. [2]

Poetry in the prophetic books is harder to see. Robert Lowth's series of published Oxford lectures appealed to his contemporary and subsequent biblical scholars. His theme is that biblical prophecy was itself a form of poetry that was inspired by the Holy Spirit.[3] In response to the troublesome issue of Hebrew meter, he suggested "parallelism," the restating or reinterpreting of the initial thought in a parallel line of similar length.[4]

A time-honored definition of prophet that eschews a predictive role is "spokesperson for God," like a messenger to a king. "We have not listened to your servants the prophets, who spoke in your name to our kings, our princes, and our ancestors, and to all the people of the land" (Dan 9:6). When poets as God's spokesperson speak in poetry, God's voice comes through poetic images.

How did people of Israel understand the connection between prophet and poet?

James L. Kugel in a book he edited, *Poetry and Prophecy: The Beginnings of a Literary Tradition,* addresses that question in his essay, "Poets and Prophets." In brief, he said that in the eyes of early Judaism and in the classic rabbinical writings, from the second to sixth century CE, song was held in great esteem, but any association of Divine Word with mere song was offensive.[5] There was little interest in poetic structure.[6] My general observation is, what preacher wants to play second fiddle to the choir? More academic types may see things differently. Take Philo for example.

In late antiquity, according to Kugel, Philo of Alexandria, "the great expositor of Hebrew Scripture," said that Moses learned rhythm and meter from the Egyptians and thus to Philo the offices of poet and prophet were not utterly foreign to each other. He goes on to say that about a century later the Jewish historian, Josephus, compared David to Greek canons of poetry.[7]

2. Wilder, *The Language of the Gospel*, 101.
3. Kugel, ed., *Poetry and Prophecy*, 22–24.
4. Ibid., 24.
5. Ibid., 10.
6. Ibid., 11.
7. Ibid., 12.

Greek influence brought an understanding of the writer who was so possessed that inspiration came easily.[8] Philo drawing upon Deuteronomy 18:18 saw prophets as being possessed by God and under divine inspiration.[9] In the same vein, Philo wrote: "For prophets are interpreters of God," and he goes on to comment on Genesis 15:12, which describes the sun going down and a deep sleep falling upon Abraham. He wrote, "When the light of God shines, the human light sets; when the divine light sets, the human dawns and rises. This is what regularly befalls the fellowship of prophets. The mind is evicted at the arrival of the divine Spirit, but when that departs the mind returns to its tenancy."[10]

Centuries later a similar kind of inspiration was attributed to Jesus. In what seems to me to be a romantic mode of thought, which values originality and inspiration, William Whallon made a case for Jesus as a poet. His argument was not so much based on parallelism, which he acknowledges,[11] but on the unique sayings of Jesus passed on by oral tradition.[12] "Jesus may be regarded as an oral poet because he used formulas that were to every appearance developed for the making of poetry in an oral culture, and also because the prose context of his poetry seems to say that he composed by the ear and mouth rather than by eye and hand."[13]

According to Whallon, Jesus quoted poetry from the Old Testament as, for example, Matthew 5:5 quoting Psalm 37:11. At a risk of oversimplifying Whallon, Jesus as a scholar quoted but as a poet was more creative in his wording in his living. One example that Whallon gives as a word pair of Jesus that was not quoted specifically from the Old Testament is Matthew 7:16.[14] "You will know then by their fruits. Are grapes gathered from thorns, or figs from thistles?" He makes a case that Jesus's instruction to love one's enemies was his own special practice.[15]

I add that perhaps Jesus's poetic insights and commitment to practice came in part through states not unlike dream states. Perhaps the experience in the wilderness was a time apart that nurtured reflection and

8. Ibid., 15.

9. Ibid., 16.

10. Ibid., 16.

11. Whallon, *Formula, Character, and Context,* 196.

12. Ibid., 193–208.

13. Ibid., 208.

14. Ibid., 206.

15. Ibid., 207.

provided prayerful states of mind that Jesus thought would benefit his followers. In any case, it seems to me that Jesus's teaching of the Lord's Prayer suggests a very relaxed and quieting interaction with God who is just Judge and poetic prophet. My sense is that when people pray the Lord's Prayer week after week in church or in private devotions there is a feeling that God is on our side. A God on our side connotes justice tempered by consideration of the human predicaments of sin and sorrow. A note of compassionate judgment comes through the Lord's Prayer as set forth by P. S. Cameron in his article, "Lead Us Not into Temptation." He concludes that the meaning of the sixth petition is, "Do not judge us according to our deserts; do not bring us to open court where the verdict would be inevitable."[16] God, for whom verdicts are not inevitable, is a just Judge with a Poet-Prophet's ability to deal with ambiguity. Jesus instructs us to pray to God, our heavenly Father, who is a just Judge and Poet-Prophet. In Jesus's prayer a masculine description of God need not limit our understanding of God because women as well as men can be just judges and poet-prophets.

If a person believes that the Bible is the inspired word of God and has also noted that the Bible is part poetry, then the equation of poet and prophet as both attributes of God's nature is logical. Since God speaks in poetry through both the prophets and Jesus, of course, God has a poet's heart. However, I believe that the conception of God as just Judge having both a poet's heart and a prophet's voice rests not so much on speech patterns but more on the prayer process revealed in embedded prayer as poetic dialogue with God. Praying the Lord's Prayer with the expectation of God's just judgment tempered with compassion is a poetic thought process that is also present in other prayers in the Bible.

The definition of poetry in *Literary Forms in the New Testament: A Handbook* by James L. Bailey and Lyle D. Vander Brock provides a working definition of poetry that suggests a poetic thought process. "Although poetry has evolved over the years, it is quite possible to give a general definition of the form that applies to both first-century and modern expressions. Two elements are central. First, poetry often employs what is called figurative language. Instead of simply stating directly the thoughts she or he wishes to convey, the poet uses word pictures, images, symbols,

16. Cameron, "Lead Us Not into Temptation," 300.

metaphors and so forth, to encourage the reader to wrestle creatively with the issues at hand."[17] Second, there is some form of sustained rhythm.[18]

Since they are created in God's image, people utilize these poetic elements both in ancient times and today. My argument is based not so much on rhythm but on metaphors, images, and dialogue, which suggest that God is open to discussion. God uses the metaphor of the shield in a vision to Abram. Further on, God again speaks in pictorial images by comparing the heirs promised to Abraham to many stars. God and Abram meet. A transcendent image of heavenly stars is God's affirming word experienced in an imminent vision. After the sun went down, God spoke prophetic words in complete sentences in a dream. As Judge, God promised judgment on the nations that will oppress Abram's heirs and peace for Abram. Philo's exposition of Genesis 15:12, with the understanding of the mind departing and the divine entering, seems remarkably close to a conception of subconscious wisdom as a gift from God emerging in dreams that can incubate images and metaphors.

Whatever editorial work went into these verses does not for me undermine credibility because I both often dream in complete sentences and believe that editorial additions can be added truth. There is something to be said for trusting in the editorial processes of biblical redactors and editors.

My contention is that if God had not engaged Abram on a deep level, Abraham might not have had the ability to wrestle with the chaos and argue with God for the sake of his people. To hold God to the metaphor of Judge of all the earth must reflect a thought process that includes dreams and poetic exploration of ambiguity and different angles.

Abraham is not the only biblical character to dialogue with God. Embedded prayer in Jeremiah reveals Jeremiah and God as poets in conversation. In Jeremiah 11:20, Jeremiah addresses God. "But you, O LORD of hosts, who judge righteously, who try the heart and the mind, let me see your retribution upon them, for to you I have committed my cause." Whether these are Jeremiah's exact words or not, they certainly convey Jeremiah's complaint about his opponents through poetry. I think that the not-so-obvious treasure in this verse is the echo of God as a just Judge with a poet's heart. Jeremiah's prayer tells us that the Lord judges righteously and tries the heart and mind. Good judges discern fairly. Poets can

17. Bailey and Vander Broek, *Literary Forms in the New Testament: A Handbook*, 76.

18. Ibid., 77.

test hearts. Like Abraham, Jeremiah as poet dares to think for himself. He questions the prevailing assumption that bad people suffer and the righteous person prospers. "Why do all who are treacherous thrive?" (Jer 12:1). Furthermore, God knows both Jeremiah's opponents and Jeremiah himself. "But you, O Lord, know me; You see me and test me—my heart is with you" (Jer 12:3). Jeremiah as poet-prophet is united with God in personal relationship and mission. A poet-prophet veering ever so slightly toward universalism, who dares to question, will not buy the Deuteronomist's hard line that suffering always equals sin.

Jeremiah's prayer reveals God as a poet with words Jeremiah relished. "Your words were found, and I ate them, and your words became to me a joy and the delight of my heart; for I am called by your name, O Lord, God of hosts" (Jer 15:16). God in turn calls Jeremiah to the responsibility to use words well. "If you utter what is precious, and not what is worthless, you shall serve as my mouth. It is they who will turn to you, not you who will turn to them" (Jer 15:19). By implication, only good poets get to be prophets. God stresses the power of persuasion: "They who will turn to you." Strong persuasive ability and God's presence will create strength to lead. "And I will make you to this people a fortified wall of bronze; they will fight against you, but they shall not prevail over you, for I am with you to save you and deliver you, says the LORD" (Jer 15:20).

Saint Paul was both a poet and a preacher who asked his people to ponder poetically. First Corinthians 13 is prayerful poetry, which invites contemplation, as well as exhortation to love. In addition in First Corinthians 13, the first three words of each verse have rhythm.[19] In Philippians 1:9–11 Paul recorded his prayer in which he prays for his people to grow in discernment, which is both a poetic and a judicial task:

> And it is my prayer that your love may abound more and more, with knowledge and all discernment, so that you may approve what is excellent, and may be pure and blameless for the day of Christ, filled with the fruits of righteousness which come through Jesus Christ, to the glory and praise of God (RSV).

The day of Christ implies a future eschatological judgment, which clearly suggests the just Judge motif. Yet this Philippians passage in connection with specification about the fruits of the Spirit in Galatians shows both poetic discernment and judicial approval working in tandem. What is this "fruit of righteousness" (or "harvest of righteousness" as translated

19. Ibid., 77

in the NRSV)? In Galatians 5:22–23 (RSV) Paul said, "But the fruit of the Spirit is love, joy, peace, patience, kindness, goodness, faithfulness, gentleness, self-control; against such there is no law." Tomes have been written discussing the meaning of "no law." I suggest that one implication of "no law" is that the vision of the just Judge with a poet's heart and a prophet's voice has been realized in part or to the degree to which Paul's prayer has been answered.

There is an inkling of judicial judgment in Paul's use of the word *approve* and poetic contemplation in his word *discernment*. The word for discernment means to perceive or apprehend by the senses. The Goodspeed translation states "have a sense of what is vital." Poets apprehend, perceive, and sense. Judges provide an examining, proving role. One Greek lexicon, abridged from Liddell and Scott's *Greek-English Lexicon* says that the noun form of determine (NRSV) and approve (RSV) means an assay, proving, examiner.[20] That definition connotes judging. Discerning and approving suggest a prayer process of Poet-Prophet discerning and a just Judge approving. In a nutshell, Paul prays that Christians will perceive poetically and judge judiciously.

Prophecy, however poetic, and judgment, however fair, do not have the last words. Paul the poet-preacher told us in 1 Corinthians 13 that "Love never ends. But as for prophecies, they will come to an end . . ." (13:8). When those who belong to Christ Jesus have experienced God's just and steadfast love, like their Hebrew ancestors, charity is realized and the need for prophecy recedes. When loving action occurs, there is reason to believe that justice will ultimately prevail, that the God who speaks from a poet's heart is indeed "the Judge of all the earth."

The metaphor of judge is explicit in Genesis. The image of a poet's heart is implicit in Genesis and throughout the Bible. Whatever the combination of directly stated and implied metaphor, I believe that the image of God as just Judge and Poet-Prophet is what G. B. Caird called "commissive" in *The Language and Imagery of the Bible*. He wrote: "Many metaphors are commissive. If I call God 'Father,' I commit myself to filial dependence and obedience." He went on to credit D. D. Evans with the name "outlook" to this type of metaphor. "I look on God as father, king,

20. Liddell and Scott, *A Lexicon*, 177.

judge, shepherd, sculptor and commit myself to the attitudes or conduct which any of these implies."[21]

What then does it mean to look upon God as just Judge and Poet-Prophet? Generally, to my mind, this metaphor suggests a God whose roles transcend sex, is just and open to hearing from articulate, persuasive people about what justice means in the present and future. As Poet, God can deal with ambiguity and encourage questions. God speaks in dreams and visions to evoke our prayers and poetic play. With a prophet's voice, God reminds us of our responsibility and the open future.

I also must answer my own question. What does it mean to me to look to God as just Judge and Poet-Prophet? To look to God, as just Judge is to promise to bring my mind and imagination to assess or judge what is fair. I must try hard to see all the angles and points of view. Questions about what is at stake for various people must be considered. Believing that God is "Judge of all the earth" promotes a sense of God's universal assessing and that judgment is in God's hands.

Contemplating the heart of Poet-God is realizing that God speaks to me through dreams and calls forth play with words. To pray to God as Poet-Prophet is to discuss and question, reflect and imagine. Considering God's prophetic word is to remain open to justice and love, truth and beauty.

God is beyond all metaphors. Yet by considering many images of God, a person will have a whole sketchbook of metaphors to draw upon at different stages of life. If, for example, I find myself in a situation that calls for dealing with ambiguity I can pull the image of God as Poet out of my inner sketchbook. If my image is sketchy, I can give it more thought and draw a more detailed portrait. To draw a picture of God from one's inner sketchbook may help make prayer more possible because an image of God drawn from life in connection with reflection on the Bible is believable. To imagine God in an image that evokes prayer is to sense God starting the conversation with the words he spoke to Abram, "Do not be afraid, I am your shield" (Gen 15:1).

21. Caird, *The Language and Imagery of the Bible*, 153.

6

God as Compassionate Editor

My hardest-earned image of God is *God as Compassionate Editor*. This metaphor was discovered in guided meditation, developed in reflection, and refined in prayer. Of course, prayer is many things, including grievance, thanksgiving, confession, and petition. Yet when the Holy Spirit prays through me to evoke my greatest ability to sort with understanding, or when quietness is focus on God that eliminates unnecessary concerns, prayer is compassionate editing.

My image, which is derived from the Bible, came through personal experience in an intuitive moment. Some years before going back to seminary I asked our pastor to guide me through a meditation. I usually prefer to keep my prayers private. This was the only one time in my life that I requested help. Such independence is not necessarily a good thing, but it does suggest that my request was urgent and that my need invited another person's insight.

I was very upset about some things said to me by a relative who, like some church people, was often critical of my ideas and seemingly lacked understanding of my physical limitations. I honestly do not remember the issue or the accusations. Cam, our pastor, suggested that I imagine myself having inside me a wise person, perhaps a wise old man or woman. I must have looked annoyed. Well, Cam, fully aware that I treasured being pen pals with Martin Marty, said, "You could imagine yourself as Martin Marty."

Oh please, I thought to myself. *Thankful as I am for Dr. Marty's caring, I would still prefer to be me.* Then I surprised myself with my next statement, "I could imagine a compassionate editor."

"Yes," replied Pastor Borton. "Martin Marty is a compassionate editor, and you are too, Sharon." After the session of prayerful sorting, Rev. Borton said he wished he had it on tape. I prayed to God as Compassionate Editor, and God as compassion entered into me and prayed through me. I learned that I did have understanding of the forces that shaped the person with negative comments, but at the same time, I had a right to my own paths and tasks.

I did not understand at the time that God as Holy Spirit was both the one to whom I prayed and the one who was also working through me. I did, however, think more about my newfound image of God. God as compassionate editor is revealed in the incarnate Jesus. Jesus was a compassionate editor, who selected and used words well. Of course, we have to thank the gospel redactors for selecting and combining his teachings. Yet Jesus had to have an editor's mind to choose the powerful, poetic words of the Beatitudes and parables. Jesus distilled the essence of his tradition. He took the best from his tradition and applied it in a new way. Love of God with heart and mind and soul and of one's neighbor as oneself, as recorded in Jesus's Great Commandment in Matthew 22:37–40, Mark 12:29–30, and Luke 10:27, is based on Deuteronomy 6:4–5. Gentle Luke recorded Jesus's greatest compassionate editing. When he felt most forsaken he still empathized with people's plight of ignorance and hardness of heart. "'Father, forgive them; for they do not know what they are doing'" (Luke 23:34). In Luke's portrait Jesus on the cross was the ultimate compassionate editor, asking God to forgive people because they and we do not know what we do. Jesus went on to discern the saving trust of the righteous thief and said, "Truly I tell you, today you will be with me in Paradise" (Luke 23:43).

My assumption is that Jesus is like God; as the Son is, so is the Father. I went to my word processor and saw how the commands in the program reflected prayer as editing. Help: Sometimes prayers for help are for clearly understood needs (as an example, for healing). Sometimes petition means that people have to figure out what is wanted or needed for self or others. Return: sometimes we have to confess and return to God. Shift: prayer asking for discernment about changes calls us to ask for God's guidance as we consider options and edit some out. Margin Release: Praise, the main purpose of prayer, sometimes requires a conscious choice of taking time to think about the reasons for giving thanks. Margins can also be the safe space in which to embrace pain in order to release the power to bless. Margin release can also be rising above our concerns to look up with love to God. Delete: Sometimes I have needed God's forgiveness. At other times God has called me to consider the plights of others without buying into their destructive ways and words and as much as possible to delete their thoughts from my heart.

Center is a multifaceted word. Of course, the purest form is centering prayer. My journal writing is another kind of centering through articulation of what is most important in the clutter of concerns that is a part of the human condition. Sometimes when I have prayed to St. Ignatius, he has been an assistant editor as I quietly seek to discern and discover.

My computer, purchased after graduation from Weston, adds another significant button. Reload or refresh. Sometimes prayer is refreshing, the reloading of inner strength.

I first shared my budding image of God as Compassionate Editor in a course, "The Psychology of Women," at Andover Newton Theological School. The professor, Dr. Brita L. Gill-Austern, asked me to give her a visual image. I said a big, pink second-grade eraser. A cute, blue smurf eraser will not do. Who could rub away their little blue friend? We all make mistakes. Erasers are part of life.

Then years later in the course "Theology of Contemplative Prayer" at Weston Jesuit School of Theology, Ff. John O'Donnell, SJ, asked the class to write a short paper on apophatic or silent, wordless prayer. I realized that my metaphor for both silent and spoken prayer is compassionate editing. That image is related to my image of God as Compassionate Editor. God is ultimately beyond all metaphors. In my sense of things, metaphors are symbols that, in the thought of Paul Tillich, participate in the reality to which they point.[1] Thus they partake of ontological reality but are not "ultimate reality" in themselves.

God as Editor-in-Chief and Compassionate Editor speaks to the faithful in words and the word. The servant in Isaiah brings God's instruction and word. "The Lord GOD has given me the tongue of a teacher, that I may know how to sustain the weary with a word" (Isa 50:4). As the gospel of John attests, Jesus is God's word (John 1:1). "And the Word became flesh and lived among us . . ." (John 1:14). God's compassion is in the heart, the center of the Bible in Psalm 78. Referring to God, the psalmist wrote, "Yet he, being compassionate, forgave their iniquity . . ." (Ps 78:38).

God gives compassion. In the spirit of the Good Samaritan, God calls us to "go and do likewise" (Luke 10:37). Compassionate editing can be done and perhaps is most often accomplished with words when people

1. Tillich, *Dynamics of Faith*, 42.

pray to God or enter into the Ignatian discernment process. However, compassionate editing can also be apophatic, a deepening of quiet trust, which is deeper than words, the storage capacity of a computer or even earthly memory. Purification in silence is a kind of editing.

The most common form of wordless prayer is meditation with mantra and breathing. It can be secular or have religious content. Meditation, regardless of the teacher or precise form, is not as inclusive as it might appear. I am one of those persons for whom long periods of meditation in the formal religious sense, not the stare into the tea cup method, is limited in value. Sitting up alertly requires a pulse beat of over forty beats a minute. Or maybe there is just something neurological that is a little different about me. I go limp and on the verge of fainting easily.

Yet I am a very quiet person, and sacred stillness makes sorting and editing more possible. As you see in the chapter "Be Still," even very short meditative breaks saying, "Be still. God is," can restore. Quiet prayer for me is like looking at Morris Louis's abstract paintings of flowing bands of color around empty, quiet space. Color memories support and sustain the soul as I empty the recycle bin of my mind. Even if bad memories come, it is better to have flashbacks in God's presence than interruption of recall at the worst possible time.

In Rockport, where we used to live and have now returned, a backyard boulder is a good place to sit, be still, and know that God is God. In Connecticut a living-room chair was the best choice. Still, most often my body goes limp in mantra or long sessions of single-word prayer. One way to avoid going limp is to knit as meditation. I am not a fancy knitter. Actually, I have knit baby blankets that the church fair cannot sell and Church World Service does not want! So it is best for me to stick to no strain on the brain knitted strips for rugs that are not unlike the strands of colors in Louis's abstracts. My normal speed is so slow that some people might think that just knitting is meditation. Perhaps this is a kind of Protestant or even secular rosary bead prayer.

That last sentence reminds me that during the spring term of '97, Sister Mary Rita and I ended up in the meditation room in St. John's Residence at the same time. She had rosary beads. I did not. The grace of quiet transcends the ways of entering into it.

Inviting the Spirit to enter and pray through me in silence is to remember Scripture, pray in the present, and look forward in hope. "Be still, and know that I am God!" (Ps 46:10). "In returning and rest you shall be saved; in quietness and in trust shall be your strength" (Isa 30:15). "Abide in me as I abide in you" (John 15:4).

Being still without saying a thing is to feel that "Underneath are the everlasting arms" (Deut 33:27 RSV). Prayerful trust, in its purest form attainable on earth, when words can be eliminated is deepest compassionate editing.

7

God as Transcendent Good Will

The Christmas of the Crystal Stars

THE CHRISTMAS OF THE crystal stars gave me gifts of natural beauty and human good will that reflect divine beauty and transcendent good will. There were microscopic seeds of hope for cosmic good will throughout my life, yet hope grew large enough for me to see it more clearly during Advent of 1980. According to A. Katherine Grieb in her "Living by the Word" meditation in *The Christian Century*, Jim Wallis of the journal, *Sojourners,* once said that hope is about "trusting God in spite of all the evidence and then watching the evidence change."[1] Advent, which is the season of hope, is a fitting time for hopefulness to enter into the world and into individuals.

After my husband, Ernest, and daughter, Amy, and I moved to my hometown following Ernest's resignation from parish ministry, I yearned for acceptance and needed more writing skills. In addition to being a wife and mother I wanted to make an artistic contribution that mattered. In the boldest moment of my life, I wrote to Dr. Martin E. Marty, and he answered. I sent him a handmade collage of blue chicory flowers, which went straight to the hospital to comfort Marty's first wife, Elsa, who was terminally ill. The painting mattered in the Marty household, and so did I. There was evidence of good will at work in the world.

On the Christmas day, which followed, the wind chill factor was thirty degrees below zero in Rockport, Massachusetts. Because the ocean was so much warmer than the air, great puffs of sea smoke rose from the water and drifted through town in millions of crystal stars. I will never

1. Grieb, "Living By the Word," 20.

forget the Christmas of the crystal stars when Dr. Marty's caring shone in me. His interest in my projects and courses is a treasure that has sustained me over the years.

My first long project, entitled *Mother Loss: Broken Selves and Saving Beauty* may be the last to be published if it is published, but for now I share highlights from that effort.

On the very day in 1984 when I set my heart on attending a course, "Women Speaking in the American Protestant Traditions," taught by Dr. Phyllis Blum Cole at Harvard Divinity School, the train bridge burned. If busses had not replaced trains, I might not have been able to get to school. Thus, I do not downplay the importance of bridges made of concrete and steel. Still, I discovered at Harvard Divinity School and later at Andover Newton Theological School and Weston Jesuit School of Theology that there are more important bridges. Soul sisters sprang from the pages of historic texts and created bridges of the heart made with stones of shared experiences of mother loss. Then Dr. Marty suggested that I as editor collect the stories of my contemporaries who as young girls had lost their mothers in death, as I had. I put research notices into religious journals, including *The Christian Century, Sisters Today, Daughters of Sarah, United Church News*, and *Good News,* a newsletter of the Universalist Unitarian Christian Fellowship.

The collective definition of God that emerged from the stories of both my historical and contemporary friends is transcendent good will. This concept is very broad and can, I believe, be accepted by both theists and non-theists. In this essay, my historical and contemporary soul sisters are all Christians who worship a personal God. Yet transcendent good will is not limited to the forgiveness of God and the nurturing of Jesus the Christ that these women came to know in their hearts.

Abstract nouns describe transcendent indices for believers and non-believers. Such abstract nouns include justice, fairness, forgiveness, beauty, and community. The word *community* may refer to specific faith groups or may be more abstract. People who believe in God and people who do not can experience good will that transcends their times and places, friends known and unknown. The gift of good will that helps people feel that the world is friendly may come at any time from anyone.

Beauty is an abstract noun of tremendous importance. Because beauty as a transcendent category presents both promise and theological problems, I wish to explore the ways in which beauty sustains, lifts us beyond ourselves, and helps people trust that the universe is ultimately a good place.

BEAUTY IN NATURE

People often speak of finding God in nature. Nature can be quieting and consoling. There is biblical precedent for sensing God in nature or the possibility that God is revealed in the created order. "Ever since the creation of the world his eternal power and divine nature, invisible though they are, have been understood and seen through the things he has made" (Rom 1:20). While for years I have not been completely comfortable with the notion of God in nature because nature can be cruel and uncaring, I have, as have countless others, felt the presence of God when pausing along life's way in a vista of beauty.

In wrestling with my apprehensions and theological problems, I wrote the following poem that suggests that beauty is the meeting ground where people and God meet or people rise above individualistic concerns.

On Tiptoe

In the darkening of dusk,
in the graying of approaching
storm, pink rose of Sharon
buds, blue bachelor
buttons and orange zinnias
soften the blackening not by
the promise of God in nature
but through connection on
the meeting ground of beauty
that stirs the imagination to
envision possibilities beyond
the self when seekers stand
on tiptoe to touch transcendence.

Sometimes nature and grace come together and through beauty lift human hearts. I wrote the following poem during our days in Meriden.

April Blessing

Robin in the snow,
I wonder if you know
the joy you bring
when you sing of spring.
Pecking through the
crusty ice, you evoke
in me fresh zest for life.
When nature and grace
                    Converge . . .
Beauty is the Word.

People need not be believers in a personal God to be uplifted by wonder and astonishment in the presence of beauty. Patrick Sherry wrote that perhaps the leading exponent of a revelatory view of beauty in the twentieth century is Simone Weil. She thought of the experience of beauty as an experience of the transcendent, more specifically an experience of God, and that for unbelievers it is a form of what she called the implicit love of God. She describes the world's beauty as "the sign of an exchange of love between the Creator and creation." Weil sees beauty as "Christ's tender smile for us coming through matter." In my summary of Weil and Sherry, human love for beauty comes from God indwelling in the soul and then that love goes out to God, who is present in the universe.[2]

My Puritan spiritual ancestor linked beauty in nature more explicitly with Christ. According to Patrick Sherry in his book, *Spirit and Beauty*, Jonathan Edwards said that when we are delighted with flowery meadows, green trees and fields, rivers and murmuring streams, singing birds, and all the other glories of nature, we should see them as "emanations of the sweet benevolence of Jesus Christ," and "shadow of his infinite beauty and loveliness."[3] Sherry goes on to explain that to Edwards, God is not only beautiful but also the source of beauty, and that in his view divine beauty differs from other kinds of beauty[4] because he is concerned with spiritual beauty and the figure of Christ revealing absolute beauty. For Edwards the divine beauty appears especially in the Son and Holy Spirit which gives heart sense to discover the glory and excellence of Christ.[5] Beauty in human life is interconnected with benevolence. Edwards found beauty in "an unrestricted benevolence of a generous heart" that flows into good will.[6]

BEAUTY IN THE ARTS

The biblical precedent for beauty in the arts is tangential and speculative. There is attention to the architecture of King Solomon's temple. Even more significant to me is the constant repetition of colors of liturgical

2. Sherry, *Spirit and Beauty*, 51.
3. Ibid., 14.
4. Ibid., 14.
5. Ibid., 15.
6. Farely, *Faith and Beauty*, 45.

vestments, blue, purple, and scarlet. Liturgy is related to the performing arts and all manner of artists and craft persons utilize color.

Sister Wendy Beckett wrote about beauty in art that enables the viewer to see beyond self. In her book *Sister Wendy's Odyssey: A Journey of Discovery*, she discusses the painting "The Gust of Wind" by Auguste Renoir, which is an oil on canvas owned by the Fitzwilliam Museum in Cambridge, England. In this small painting, which is only 20 ½ by 32 ½ inches, the wind blows through the grasses. Fluffy clouds touch the horizon. The painting evokes empathy in me because, having sat in a similar field in Rockport, I can in my mind feel the warm sunlight and gentle breezes and thus share in Renoir's morning sometime between 1872 and 1875. Sister Wendy wrote: "This small, unpretentious picture shows us what the spiritual in art is all about. Renoir takes us out of our confined, our ego-cage, into a timeless world, and our stay in it leaves us changed. It would be futile to try to say precisely how we are changed, but great art can be recognized subjectively by its effect on us. We have been enlarged in our own being by receiving the blessing of another's."[7] I believe that Sister Wendy's thoughts converge with my poem, experience, and even paintings of fields in Rockport.

BEAUTY IN COMMUNITY

Life in community can be beautiful. There is biblical precedent for the beauty of service. In Matthew's story of the anointing at Bethany, an unnamed woman poured a very costly ointment onto Jesus's head (Matt 26:6–13). The disciples were annoyed and asked, "Why this waste when the ointment could have been sold and the money given to the poor?" But Jesus noted the anger that may have been at the root of their question and said that the woman had done a good service for him. The Revised Standard Version states: "'Why do you trouble this woman? For she has done a beautiful thing to me'" (Matt 26:10). The New Revised Standard Version states, "Why do you trouble this woman? She has performed a good service for me" (Matt 26:10). New Testament Greek is a highly nuanced language. There can be many translations for words and the backgrounds of words have multiple layers. The New Testament Greek word *kalos* can mean good, right, proper, fitting, better, honorable, honest, fine, beautiful, or precious.

7. Beckett, *Sister Wendy's Odyssey*, 34.

In my sense of things, both translations taken together suggest the interconnection of the good and beautiful in Christian service. Furthermore, *kalos* as it is used in the preaching of the gospel in Matthew, Mark, and Luke is orientated to the message of the kingdom of God.[8] Therefore beauty and goodness are dimensions of God's reign.

Early mother loss leads to doubt that the world is friendly. Yet in time the women in my collection grew in trust that God wills them well and went on to create lives of beauty in their faith communities and in various callings, including the arts. W. W. Meissner summarized the impact of early mother loss. He wrote that the gist of loss is that the early loss of a parent can cast a shadow across the entire life course of a child.[9] Women who lost their mothers at an early age and told me their stories tend to be somber and serious yet open to light and love.

In his book *A Cry of Absence: Reflections for the Winter of the Heart,* Martin E. Marty paints a picture of serious souls that coordinates with the stories in this chapter. Dr. Marty recalls an interview with Karl Rahner and his discussion between summery and wintry types of religious outlooks. While these types are not chemically pure, the distinctions are worth noting. Summery Christians are smiling and confident. Wintry sorts are somber. They can understand atheistic doubts while still sustained by a *yes*. The paternal heart of God promised care but seems uncaring. Summery-style people storm that heart and expect it to be heated and open. The winter-type people storm and find a more distant heart and a less warm response but still a response. [10]

In this essay I will tell the story of two historical soul sisters and two contemporary friends who found their ways of embracing transcendent good will and went on to create lives of beauty in their faith communities. Because mother loss so deeply hurt, their religious convictions are never facile. Historical soul sister Jane Holmes and contemporary friend Meg both needed the experience of forgiveness in order to experience God's good will. Moravian historical friend Martha Powell and Loulla, who is my contemporary, both found meaning and mutual good will in their Christian communities and missionary service. Not only do Loulla and

8. Kittel, *Theological Dictionary of the New Testament Vol. III,* 545.

9. Meissner, *Ignatius of Loyola,* 9.

10. Marty, *A Cry of Absence,* 10–12.

Meg live in ways that beautify faith communities, Loulla also participates in beauty through gardening and Meg through photography.

HISTORICAL FRIEND JANE HOLMES

Jane Holmes, Puritan friend from the seventeenth century who died in 1653, was the first historical friend I met in a Harvard Divinity School course, "Women Speaking in the American Protestant Traditions," taught by Dr. Phyllis Blum Cole. I sensed right away that her whole spirituality sprang from the death of her mother and the resultant need to find love, acceptance, and warmth within a family circle. As her life unfolded, she would also need forgiveness, which is kin to acceptance.

After her mother died, Jane did not have the comfort of family with her stepmother and new siblings. God's love was eclipsed by the shadow of loss. Jane made the most of a bad situation by reading the Bible, a time-honored Protestant approach. She also looked to her Puritan church in England, which did not meet her needs. She tried harder by following some of the faithful to New England. She was sexually abused on board ship. Jane Holmes, now Goodwife Jane Holmes, told her story to her pastor.

In seventeenth-century Congregationalism, people told their spiritual story or made their confession before becoming church members. Jane told her story, which was recorded by her pastor, the Reverend Thomas Shepard, and is now in the book, *Thomas Shepard's Confessions,* by George Selement and Bruce C. Wooley and published in 1981 by The Colonial Society of Massachusetts. She said she believed that God would redeem her token of troubles as the Biblical Tamar of Genesis 38 had her tokens claimed by her father-in-law. Jane did not have children, which would have given her meaning and value in her community. As you recall, Tamar felt worthless because she was not given her late husband's brother for her new mate as was the custom. Taking action, Tamar tricked her father-in-law into intercourse. Tamar was given a ring and card, instead of a goat, for payment. She proved that her father-in law had been intimate by producing the tokens. At first the older man planned revenge but then proclaimed, "She is more righteous than I" (Gen 38:26 RSV).

In times of trouble, sustaining images descend into deep interior places. Jane's appropriation of Tamar's tokens of trouble must have given her strength to proceed in trust that eventually God would prove her goodness and make his love felt.

After hearing a sermon about contentment from relying on the Lord, Jane said, "And that I found . . . and will not the Lord own those tokens and are these nothing? So I. And finding a rebellious heart, by many trials I found Lord in me and I found Lord. I loved Him and I found that my grief was that sin parted between me and God. And on Sabbath Day morning . . . I found Lord persuaded my heart of His love."[11] This high point on her spiritual journey is mystical and mighty, powerful and persuasive.

Jane does not explicitly say that her grief was her sin but that is one implication. Whether her sin is her past, her grief or a combination of both the working out of grief made room for contentment. Her story shows how images may take root in the soul, grow and flower into feelings of certainty.

MEG, JANE'S CONTEMPORARY SOUL FRIEND

Meg was a terrible teenager, but when her mother developed cancer, Meg's life started to turn around. Like her historical soul mate Jane Holmes, Meg needed forgiveness, although, of course, she did not yet know that when she first learned of her mother's diagnosis. I quote from the tape recording that she dictated for me around 1986.

> In my senior year in high school, I went to my grandmother's home on Cape Cod next to which we had a little summerhouse. The cottage hadn't opened for the summer. I arrived with a group of friends. We stayed up all night drinking and broke into the summerhouse after dark when we could not be seen from my grandmother's large, rambling house where my parents stayed. The next morning I had to explain to my parents what had gone on, why we weren't back at my grandmother's by midnight, and why we broke into the summer house. They looked at me and said, "Oh." I thought this was strange because usually they would have been furious. I usually got hell and would be grounded for a thing like that. This time they acted like it wasn't really important. I knew something was up.
>
> A little later that day they said we were going to walk down to the beach for a "family talk," which terrified me because we almost never had "family talks." The only other time this had happened was when my parents, separated at one point, announced that they were getting back together. I remember thinking all the serious

11. Selement and Wooley, *Confessions*, 80.

decisions in life had been made on the beach. When we were on the beach, my mother said, "I want you to know that I have cancer." The world turned upside down.

This was more serious than anything I ever had to deal with before. I suddenly realized that I could no longer rely on my parents to give me everything. They weren't going to be with me forever. It was about time I grew up, turned around, and did something for them, which was very difficult, as I was entirely self-centered. I remember walking back up the hill from the beach. I took my mother's arm, something I had never done before. I had never made a gesture of love toward her since I was little. It was an attempt to comfort her, knowing that she really needed it at that time. I had never done anything selfless before in my life that I can remember. We just walked up very quietly from the beach. That was one of those moments that changed my life.

Still being a mixed-up teenager, I mostly tried to deny what was happening. I had a very difficult time with her dying process, seeing her become worse and not knowing what to say or do. I felt needy and knew that I could no longer just be needy. It was time to do something else, yet I stayed away from my mother a lot out of fear and denial.

Toward the end of that fearful year, Meg left for college.

I was in art school, sharing a house with three other girls from school. I would go down to see my mother at Massachusetts General Hospital in Boston about once a month. She then moved to a hospital in Connecticut when my dad was transferred there. He bought a house two blocks from the hospital. She was home a little but in the hospital most of the time. That she was really dying became clear. The cancer spread everywhere; there was just no hope.

I often went to Connecticut with my older sister. We had been visiting more frequently, and it was early April when my mother went into a coma. She probably would not wake up before she died. It was just a matter of days or, at most, two weeks. Sitting in the hospital room seemed pointless when my mother was unconscious, or if she was awake, she didn't know who we were being so delirious from the pain and medication. I was totally confused. When she slipped into the final coma, my dad said, "I'11 take you back to school. I'll call you when it's over."

He drove my sister and me back to college. We left my sister at Wellesley around midnight, and my father dropped me off in

> Gloucester around one o'clock. Then he had to drive five more hours back to Connecticut. He was on the road for ten hours.
> I stayed up the whole night and could not justify being away at that time. I sat up to write a song for my mother. I played the guitar, trying to find a way to grieve and to say that I loved her. When I couldn't stand it anymore, I called my sister in the morning and said, "I'm going to get on the first train that goes into Boston, and then I'm taking Amtrak. I want you to meet me on the 1:28 train." So we did.
>
> We arrived at my father's house. He was furious because he had driven ten hours to take us back to school, and there we were in his doorstep again. He couldn't get rid of us. Even though he was angry, I know he appreciated our being there. My mother had worsened. I brought my guitar and the song I had written. If there was any chance I could sing this love song to my mother or my father, I would.
>
> We went back to the hospital in the late afternoon. She was still comatose. We went home and had dinner. When my father, sister, and I returned to the hospital, she was awake, propped up on her pillow, alert, and without pain for the first time in months! She was coherent—not that she said much, but she was there. She was completely clear. She knew me and smiled at me as a mother smiles, lovingly at her child.
>
> At the time I didn't recognize this as a gift from God, but I did recognize this as my opportunity. It took every ounce of courage I had, but I sang the song to her. My father and sister were there. Dad sat on Mom's bed and held her hand. His eyes were filled with tears. I finished the song and put the guitar away. My mom smiled lovingly at me. I knew her love covered a multitude of my sins. The past no longer mattered. She forgave me.
>
> If this God-given opportunity had not happened, I would have spent the rest of my life feeling guilty that I had been so awful to her. It must have been God who prompted me to write the song, and for her to forgive me. It was the first time that I knew unconditional love and forgiveness. It was as though I had seen Christ, but I didn't know that yet.

Meg's maternal grandmother was not as forgiving. Meg took on the guilt and blamed herself for her grandmother's dislike and lack of understanding. In time Meg experienced the inclusiveness of God's forgiveness. "What I know now is that God forgives us even when people don't. It is a very real and tangible forgiveness. You may not be able to make up for the wrongs you have done, but you can be forgiven. Since that experience, God's grace has created countless opportunities for me. The forgiveness of God has helped me deal with all my guilt. I feel remorse about some of the things I have done, but I don't have to continue punishing myself because I can't make up for them. I am sorry and I am forgiven. My mother's illness and death were turning points in my life. I know that God must exist. He provided that most grace-filled moment in my life. Without this grace, I could have remained a guilty person, punishing myself forever."

As a teenager Meg did not like children because she did not like herself as a child. As a mother her priorities changed, and she found a model in memories of her mother. When her children were young, she was home when they came home from school. "My mother always was. I remember the secure feeling of flinging open the door and saying, 'Mom, I'm home.' From some other part of the house I'd hear her saying, 'Hi, how was your day?' Loving presence gives you a firm foundation, something to go back to when you are older.

"A mother's presence is almost spiritual; there is something going on that has no words. When you've grown, when that presence is taken away before its natural conclusion, how do you fill that void? As I've grown older I realize that I've spent fourteen years looking for a mother." Meg began to realize that the void, that need for a nurturing presence, an unseen, unspoken bond, was being replaced with Christ.

Only the mothering, nurturing aspect of Christ could fill the emptiness. Meg wants her children to know without having to learn the hard way that the maternal relationship can be replaced by one with Christ at some point.

> We do have an eternal spiritual parent. God, through Christ, takes care of that need. He wants to be our parent, and we can depend upon him totally. He never lets us down. He always loves us, comforts us, forgives us, and helps us back upon our feet.
>
> Before my mother died, I had been very interested in art. I have since worked as a nurse's aide and in human services. At first I wanted to do something in the health profession to deal with my own sense of helplessness at not being able to help my mother. One time when she was sick at home, the visiting nurse called to say she couldn't come in. I heard the bell next to her bed ring to summon aid. I went into her room and she said, "The nurse won't be in today and I need you." That was the first time I was able to physically minister to my mother. She was throwing up due to her chemo-

> therapy and radiation treatments and I held the basin, tending to all those things that really disgusted me. I cooked dinner that night for the first time. My mother tried to tell me how to do it from her bed. It tasted awful. She tried to eat it anyway and praised me.
>
> For the first time God had shown me that I had other gifts. I could minister to someone else. After my mother died, I became a nurse's aide in a nursing home. I was later accepted into a nursing program at the local hospital. I was all ready to go when I discovered that I was pregnant, so I withdrew my application.
>
> I worked, took care of my children, and put my husband through school.

Some years ago Meg went back to school and took some photography courses. She did a mother/daughter series and said at the time, "I am finding many creative ways to make something beautiful out of this loss."

Meg summarizes in these words: "God can redeem even that which is clearly bad. As terrible as the loss of my mother was, God's hand was clearly there, and so much good has come from those few moments of grace. Although I am terrified of suffering, I am not afraid of death. On her deathbed, my mother showed me the gift of unconditional love and forgiveness that Christ has for me, and I have turned to Christ to fill my innermost needs. Without Him I would still be in constant torment and guilt for all the things I have done and continue to do that cause harm. It would be hell on earth. Now I have hope that even though my mother and I never discussed faith, she will be waiting for me in heaven. I will be able to tell her again someday how much I love her and thank her for her final gift to me that eventually released me from terrible bondage. But it was God's grace that provided the opportunity. He deserves constant thanks as he continues to bless me with moments of grace that shine a light on the path to lead me out from the darkness."

Meg's story presents Jesus as the fullest sign of God's transcendent good will, which is personalized and made incarnate in a nurturing, mothering Christ. Her testimony is sign that God is.

ADDENDUM

Just before I submitted my manuscript to the copy editor, Meg learned that she has been accepted to a nursing school thirty-six years after she needed to withdraw her first application. Dreams coming true are a big hint that God is and that God guides. Nurses provide caring that is a reflection of God's love.

MARTHA POWELL HISTORICAL FRIEND

Historical friend Martha Powell was born in 1704. She shows us the beauty in Christian community. Martha's most complete story can be found in the book, *Women and Religion in America Volume 2: The Colonial and Revolutionary Periods* edited by Rosemary Radford Ruther and Rosemary Skinner Keller. Martha Powell was born in England and lived an ordinary life. Like other members of Moravian congregations, she wrote a spiritual biography that was completed by her pastor at the time of death. Martha's mother was a Quaker and concerned for the salvation of her children. Her father was a more worldly man. Martha, who lost her mother when she was five, said that she was quite taken up with the pleasures of the world. Yet she reported that she nevertheless frequently melted into Tears when she heard at church of the Savior's sufferings. Her use of capital letters emphasizes the emotional impact. I believe that this identification with the suffering Jesus enabled Martha to embrace grief, probably in the intermittent way of children, and to move on to assurances of God's good will as well as choosing later to follow her mother's faith in another and more warmly demonstrative faith community.

Martha shared a crucial religious experience, which was also an aesthetic experience. Beauty came in the form of Christ's sacrificial love. Martha wrote: "One time 14 of us being at a Love Feast, Brother Wing at the close of the Meeting fell on his knees and pray'd more fervently. In that Instant my dear Savior! My Lord and My God! drew near my heart in his bleeding Form, and it was to me as tho he spoke audibly to me: 'I have loved thee with an everlasting Love and none shall pluck thee out of my hand.'" [12] Her crucial words, "as tho" make it clear that she is not talking about hearing voices but receiving inner auditory conviction. Martha's religious experience in a worship service that was fellowship of faith gave her peace and deep conviction of God's presence.

Martha's use of the words "Form" and "Love," which are both capitalized to stress their importance, suggests to me that Martha had a feeling akin to a classical understanding of Platonic eternal realities that merged with seeing beauty in the form of Christ's sacrificial love as did Jonathan Edwards. Thus Christ's suffering perfects and gives her peace with her own pain. Love and service in Christian community are reflections of divine love, suffering, and beauty.

12. Reuther and Keller, *Women and Religion in America,* Vol. 2, 295.

Martha worked for a while among the single Moravian Sisters. Then, at age thirty-eight, she married Joseph Powell. The Powells sailed from England to their new faith community in Bethlehem, Pennsylvania. Martha was very much a part of community meetings. She said that grace that reigned in the growing congregation made her willing to assist. Martha and her husband gave years of service for their beloved congregation, including several missionary journeys through the colonies and to Jamaica. Earthly fellowship participated in eternal fellowships of all the saints at rest.

LOULLA, MARTHA'S CONTEMPORARY SOUL FRIEND

Like Martha, Loulla found God's loving good will in Christian communities and has worked hard to make life beautiful for other people. Loulla's life journey thus far has taken her from the island of Cyprus to the Ozarks in Missouri to a growing suburb of Kansas City. During her formative years she was a faithful Christian in the Greek Orthodox tradition. As a Southern Baptist, she is equally steadfast in the Christian way of life. Today, in addition to attending church, she helps the youth director with mission trips.

Loulla has experienced valleys of loneliness, ridicule, and rejection yet also high-points when she knows God's saints have been there for her. "There is always someone there to help," she said. As a child, school was often a struggle. Over time, difficulties in learning made her a better teacher. Before retirement in 2003, Loulla was a sixth grade teacher and one of the best teachers in the school system, according to a neighbor who was also a teacher in the 1980s when I first interviewed Loulla.

Retirement gave Loulla time to have fun. She joined bridge groups and a hand-bell choir. As a child she did not have an instrument, so she is excited about now being in charge of four bells. Ever since we first met I have felt a kinship with Loulla. We were born in the same year, lost our mothers in childhood, and had difficulties in school. However, I did not know until writing this book how much we have in common about spelling. Loulla was afraid that some parents would find out about her not-always-accurate spelling, and until recently I have been very nervous when writing because of my spelling. Some time ago I had a dream in which I told my high school English teacher that spelling is not the only measure of intelligence. In the dream she agreed. That dream marked a turning point for me. Both Loulla and I hope that parents will not label children as stupid who just do not hear in a way that aids spelling.

When I first interviewed Loulla, she was very involved in the Women's Missionary Union (WMU) of her church, especially the teenage division, where she introduces young girls to the program. She took the girls on numerous missionary errands where the emphasis is helping people in need. Loulla and other women in the WMU minister through their presence and support.

Over twenty years ago, in addition to her work with very young women, Loulla was also in charge of establishing WMUs in small, new, ethnic churches. The Southern Baptist Convention (SBC) is not known for being on the front lines of women's liberation. Yet because the ethnic churches had large proportions of men who dominate their wives, formations of WMU groups in these churches brought new autonomy to many women. These women, who meet for a common cause, found support that comes from sharing concerns and bonding together in Christian service.

With all the change in Loulla's life, one might expect a story of discontinuity. Instead, hers is a story of continuity of the passing of spiritual gifts from mother to daughter. Like the little edelweiss in the song of the same name from Loulla's favorite movie, *The Sound of Music*, Loulla's caring and compassion will "bloom and grow forever." These qualities are shared and thus re-seed and flower.

Loulla was born in Cyprus in 1944. Her father was her mother's second husband. When Loulla's mother's first husband died, she was financially well off, although she was emotionally burdened by the loss of five children who had died before age thirteen. She was afraid that Loulla would die also, although Loulla did not know about her mother's fears until many years later. The stories Loulla heard from her mother were not tales of sorrow and mistrust but testimonies to trust, thanksgiving, courage, and praise.

Loulla's father left when she was six months old. Before he deserted his family, he sold all the remaining embroidery that Loulla's mother had fashioned and that her first husband had sold in America at large profits. The family was no longer well to do. Like most other children, Loulla wanted things that were not affordable. Her mother would say, "Look at what we have. We have a house and plenty to eat. We can buy meat." Loulla's mother also told stories about the value of work and determination. Loulla's mother set an example. At age thirty-five she learned to read in order to write letters to her first husband when he was on business trips. She learned just enough to manage. "She was an older woman who did what was necessary. Her message was clear, 'You can do it if you try—at least enough to get by.'" Independence was her watchword.

Biblical stories as well as a work ethic gave Loulla direction. Because Jesus ate in the fields, it was generally concluded that it was not unlawful for people to eat from the fields, although it was wrong to bring produce home. Despite the belief that if people worked, they would not go hungry, Loulla's mother fed many people. "That was the story of the Good Samaritan," said Loulla. "Everything we did was centered on the Bible and religion." God was understood as taking a very active part in human life. "Trust God and everything that happens will turn out for the best. God will take care of you. He has His hand on you," affirmed Loulla's mother when Loulla just missed being bitten by a scorpion in a field far from medical help.

Loulla's village church was Christ Church. Churches celebrated the saint's day of their name. So, twice a year there was "Christ Day." One ritual presented some problems for Loulla. Chickens were sprinkled and blessed with holy water. Christ is powerful, and Loulla believed in that strength. Water that touched the cross was holy. But what if all the chickens were not sprinkled? Some of the water flowed away. Loulla asked questions. "We do it because it works," said her mother. Loulla adopted the faith in essence if not detail.

Mary, mother of Jesus, was important to Loulla's mother. In fact, Loulla's mother said, "Mary is a woman. She understands us better." Many prayers were offered through Mary. Loulla had not been able to make much sense over the division in the SBC over the ordination of women. Although men and women were separated in the Orthodox tradition, explained Loulla, "We had Mary." Mary was a powerful symbol of understanding for Loulla's mother and a hint of generous good will for Loulla.

A tremendous spirit of compassion comes through the stories Loulla's mother told about her second husband. "He is a good man, so talented. If it were not for his bad habits of drinking and gambling, he would be with us and provide."

During their village days, Loulla's mother worried about Loulla's schoolwork. Loulla repeated sixth grade. Today she holds a master's degree in mathematics. As a child she got into mischief typical of many children with learning problems. She also learned embroidery and the joy of making an attractive home. Her mother lost interest in the house. "She was only interested in living and taking care of me." Loulla whitewashed the house. She consolidated the woodpiles and planted flowers. Lining the hallways with potted plants, she gave love to both home and mother.

Then, when Loulla was fifteen, her mother died of a stroke. Loulla stayed in the house for three days. Then she called her aunt and uncle to come and get her. "Oh, do you want us to?" they asked. From the perspective of age forty-two, Loulla was grateful her aunt and uncle took her into their home. In class-conscious Greece it was not easy to take in a niece with a village accent who was having trouble in school. Her aunt and uncle paid for boarding school. They understood the importance of getting ahead and being able to speak English. Loulla's uncle was born into a small village and earlier in life was considered lower class. In his village he worked extremely hard selling olive oil. He also learned English and opened a city factory making soft drinks that included lemonade, cherry soda, and orange drink. Exporting carob was another enterprise. Loulla admired his ability to prosper and reach a higher class. Her mother had often told her, "Accept who you are and be proud, but you can always better yourself."

At school Loulla was lonely when friends went home for the weekends. She missed out on shopping trips and experienced the humiliation of repeating a grade. Then, all of a sudden things clicked. Loulla greeted her teacher in English. Learning became fun. She had a taste of success. Teachers liked her. At the end of her first successful school year, she was told she could skip a year with just a little work over the summer.

Advancing that fast was not to be. Loulla's new family had many summer visitors. Not being accepted in the household as upper class, Loulla was expected to work along with the servants doing household tasks. Another stumbling block was that her aunt and uncle were not in favor of her returning to school. She was told, "You know all the English you need to know." For the first time in her life, Loulla talked back, reminding her aunt she could have skipped a grade if there had been time to study. She returned to school.

Still, Loulla considers her aunt and uncle to be saintly. Another saint who did not turn out to be perfect was there to help for a while. Loulla became close to one of the teachers, June, who invited Loulla to go to America, all expenses paid, for three years on condition that Loulla return to Greece as a Protestant missionary. "I will never give up my religion,"

Loulla stated, feeling sure the offer would be withdrawn. "That's okay," June said, still offering the gift of America and holding on to the hope that Loulla would become a missionary.

Her aunt and uncle discussed the matter. Everyone thought it would be a great chance for Loulla. After discovering that instead of the school sending Loulla it would be June, her aunt and uncle almost withdrew their permission. However, they had already told people in Loulla's native village about her educational opportunity. They did not wish to disappoint the villagers, who cared deeply for Loulla.

In America, Loulla went to school and attended the Reformed Presbyterian Church. She deeply admired June for putting her faith into action. "After church she would look around to see who was alone and invite them to dinner." Such hospitality and biblically centered faith seemed like her mother's village faith.

One day another teacher gave Loulla a ride home. She asked about Loulla's college plans. "What's wrong with the College of the Ozarks?" her driver asked.

June wanted Loulla to return to Cyprus even if she could not be a teaching missionary because she felt a responsibility to return Loulla to her relatives. Going back was inevitable and not without some attractions. Graduating from an American high school meant that Loulla could expect to marry into the finest family. Marriage was very appealing.

Loulla went to work in Cyprus teaching kindergarten. When a missionary invited Loulla to a Protestant church, the aunt and uncle knew they and Loulla must talk. Loulla's attraction to Protestant teachings and her inner conviction that she wanted to go to America compelled her to seek more education and religious choice.

"What do you expect to do?" they asked, knowing Loulla was determined to be Protestant. "Go to the College of the Ozarks," replied Loulla. "With what?" asked her aunt and uncle. Used to sending their children to expensive schools, they were not prepared for a school where students could earn their own way. Loulla had her teaching money for transportation.

In her native village, Loulla had prayed before traditional icons. In another simple village, life in the community of the College of the Ozarks, there were real-life icons, people who offered the help that is an echo of God's graciousness. The Davidsons, who lived in Branson, a town about three miles away from the college, befriended her and gave her money for books. The first gift was twenty dollars when Loulla needed eighteen.

Bowls of fruit, which she loved, were brought to the dormitory. She and other foreign students were invited into the Davidsons' home for the holidays. Once again the people who gave time and concern were Protestant Christians.

In keeping with the prophet Haggai's exhortation, Loulla worked and trusted in God. She was offered a job in the Davidsons' jewelry store that at the time was the only one in town. At the time, Loulla thought that the Davidsons were rich but later learned that Mr. Davidson's salary was that of a first-year teacher. He himself worked against all odds. After being in an accident at age twelve, he had thirty-six surgeries. He and his wife, Pauline, had five children. The children are now all doing well. Mrs. Davidson in her eighties lives comfortably in her home. Besides being icons in real life, Mr. Davidson was and Mrs. Davidson continues to be God's jewelry, signs that God is. Jewelry sold in the store and being like God's signet ring both add beauty and sparkle to life.

After graduating from college, Loulla moved to Liberty, which is a suburb of Kansas City, Missouri. At first she was very lonely. After joining a church, she found friends and sustaining church tasks to complement her work as a teacher. She now sees her initial loneliness as experiences enabling her to be more sensitive to people who are alone.

In a letter written to me around 1986 she said, "This year I have concentrated my WMU work with the ethnic churches in the Kansas City area. What a monumental task! I am over and over reminded of my first years in the United States. As I observe these people, I am reminded of my early struggles and frustrations as I tried to learn the language, culture, customs, while all along wanting to hang on to my own . . . the familiar . . . but now strange. How can one express one's concerns when she or he cannot communicate? Yet communication is essential to survival. Frustrations skyrocket and many times it is easier to close the door to the outside world.

"I always attribute my survival to my strong Christian upbringing and high goals. Oh, how my heart goes out to these people, how I want to tell them about WMU and that there are individuals who can help them right now. It is difficult to see people struggle through life, yet it is only after we rise above those struggles that we are able to grow, mature, and become the persons God wants us to become."

What aspects of Greek Orthodoxy were still important to Loulla over twenty years ago? "Everything except kissing icons," she said. She went back to Cyprus and attended a service. "Everything was beautiful." As a child she had not realized that her religion was a faith of continual praise. She visited the people in her village and explained her faith. The townspeople found her story beautiful. Another aunt said, "I will see your mother before you do and I will tell her."

Loulla knows the peace of the conviction that her mother would be proud of her. After all, Loulla is a woman with faith in God and praise in her heart, just like her mother. Over twenty years ago when I first interviewed Loulla in her home, she summed up her message by saying, "Mothers can do something for their children by teaching them faith." Passing on faith is claiming the power to be God's signet ring. Over the years she has grown in appreciation. "How grateful I am to God for giving me that saintly mother. She taught me what I need to know to become an independent individual in this world. There is not a day that goes by when I do not think of my mother and her unconditional love."

Remembering how hard learning can be, Loulla now supports herself as a missionary. Like Martha Powell and her husband, Loulla makes missionary journeys. "Helping people is what it is all about," she said. She expects in the coming year to go to India to help with a village school. People sometimes ask her, "Why India?" She says, "I relate so much to those people and someone always stepped up to help me. Now it is my time to help others. Can you imagine if every time I visit a school at least one child is encouraged and sees his or her potential and surfaces?" Because I, like Loulla, value teachers who have believed in us, I can emphatically say that saving people from drowning in feelings of inadequacy is holy work.

Frugal as ever, Loulla grows her vegetables in Missouri and accepts gifts of deer meat in hunting season. "The entire backyard of my house is a garden. Spring is when the brown dirt begins to bring forth textures and colors. The fruit trees come to life with delightful flowers. Every day my neighbors and I enjoy the changes that take place in the garden. My little garden not only feeds me all year, but I also have enough to share with friends. What a beautiful country we live in."

Faith and trust flower as assurance that God and life will us well. In turn, Loulla is a sign that God is. Life in service to the world community can be beautifying, as can participation in homemaking, gardening, and teaching. Beauty in worship lifts the hopeful heart to God. Praise in many faith traditions with intrinsic value of enjoying God is an earthly vista of transcendent beauty.

8

Envisioning God through Biblical Color Images

People who experience joy in color may find that biblical color images strengthen their faith in God. When the essence of God is suggested by jewel tones such as sapphire and emerald, people who understand themselves as created in God's image can believe that they can be God's jewelry.

At age three I started on my journey to discovery of the importance of color in life and biblical literature. At that time I was cared for by my grandmother (whom everyone called Bessie) and her best friend, Katie, because my mother was dying from leukemia. Grandmother Bessie was an outspoken atheist. Katie was a warm-hearted evangelical Protestant. They constantly talked about religion. In retrospect, I wanted to be in on the discussion.

Even though my mother was very weak, she colored with me. My favorite crayon was the bright blue one. Light filtered through small cobalt blue vases on the windowsill and soothed my shaken self. Blue light was a nonverbal parable of God's comfort and grace. That import was revelatory and instructive. Beauty mattered.

Truth also mattered. My father, following the conventional wisdom of many in his day, did not want anyone to talk with me about death. The Universalist minister who visited the preschool group I attended at the church was the only adult in the mix willing to talk about death. I can still remember playing with blocks on the floor while talking. Truth and beauty are aesthetic dimensions of religious experience. Unlike my block houses, which toppled, truth and beauty do not. I must have sensed that truth and beauty are eternal. Early religious experience was the foundation for my adult interests.

Repression was one ingredient of my discovery of the importance of blue in life and biblical literature. This realization was a long time coming, but when it finally came, it felt eruptive, like a conversion experience. After my mother died when I was three and a half, I moved in with my older half-brother and his wife who brought me up as a favor to my father. They certainly encouraged my interest in art but were understandably not perceptive enough to understand why a four-year-old was so preoccupied with the color blue.

"Someday I want to live in a blue house."

"Oh no, houses are not blue."

"Well, blue shutters."

"No, blue fades too easily. We have heard enough about blue."

Ceasing to talk about blue did serve me well in the long run.

I forgot about blue for a long time. For the first decade of our married life, my husband was a parish minister. As a young minister's wife, I wrote in my journal (which I called "Reflections of a Minister's Wife") that, while blue had never been my favorite color, I really liked our parsonage bedroom wallpaper with blue flowers on a white background. Years later while reading my journal I said to myself, "What? Remember the blue vases. Remember your sixth grade Easter dress that was white with a blue print and blue sash. You have always liked blue."

My new family did not understand my interest in religion either. Nature pushed. Grace pulled. As a result, I majored in art and had minors in English and religion at Albion College. Thirty years later I had a biblical concentration at Weston Jesuit School of Theology. Eventually I would see that color in the Bible is revelatory. Bold as it is, I paint abstract pictures symbolic of what God might look like based on biblical passages where color is part of theological import.

There are four basic points about the role of color in the Bible.

1. Considering biblical color images of God addresses the problem of how to picture God when graven images are prohibited.
2. Color in the Bible is revelatory because biblical color words suggest abstract images of God.
3. The aesthetic theories of Wassily Kandinsky and theological writings of Paul Tillich explain how biblical color conveys revelatory images through associative connotations and symbolic import.
4. An abstract image of God in *Revelation* is a first-century subversion of patriarchy.

By discussing color in the Bible and how I use it to paint abstract pictures of what God could look like, I am here addressing how color in the Bible speaks about the nature of God and also may suggest the voice of God. Witness of color through direct description of God's habitation or allusion to God's being is ontologically significant. When color is part of the meaning and end of life, color has teleological import.

I am not the only artist to conclude that God may speak through colors as well as words to the biblical writers. In a seventeenth-century Armenian manuscript, a painter, Mesrop of Khizan (1615) painted a picture of St. John called "Saint John the Evangelist" to illuminate a Gospel book *Isfahan,* written by Hayrapet, which is owned by the J. Paul Getty Museum.[1]

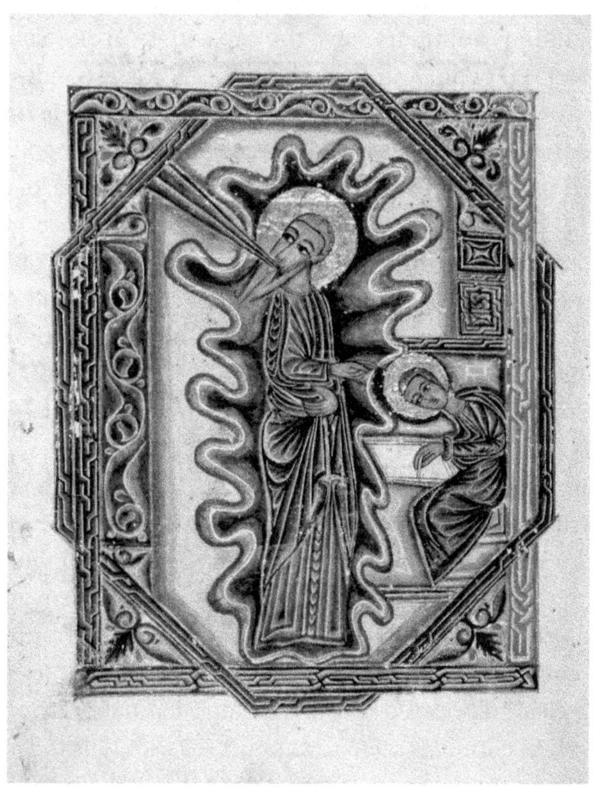

God's dwelling is implied as existing outside the frame-like structure. God's words in the form of blue rays flow from God into St. John's

1. J. Paul Getty Museum, MS. Ludwig II 7, fol.193v.

mouth. The implication is that God speaks from a transcendent realm and is revealed in colors, especially blue.

The writings of theologian Paul Tillich and abstract painter Wassily Kandinsky add to my understanding of why color in the Bible is revelatory and how color can communicate. In my aesthetic reading of the Bible, color symbolically reveals God's attributes and actions. Symbols, as Paul Tillich pointed out in his classic book, *Dynamics of Faith,* participate in the reality to which they point.[2]

It seems to me that the aesthetic theories of Wassily Kandinsky explain how biblical references to color function as symbols of God's being and attributes. Kandinsky developed his ideas in a book, *Concerning the Spiritual in Art.* He believed that a work of art consists of both an inner and outer element.[3] The inner element is the emotions in the souls of artists that in my summary have the capacity to evoke a similar emotion in the observer, or in Kandinsky's words "a corresponding vibration of the human soul.[4] Thus there is a spiritual reality that is understood and expressed in non-figurative visual language. In an analogous way, I believe that some biblical authors expressed understandings of God through color words that symbolize God's purity, power, presence, glory, and light. If biblical readers find symbolic meaning in the color words in the Bible, the writers artistically communicated their emotions and inner visions. I suggest that when biblical writers express God though color, they are akin to Kandinsky.

Of course, Kandinsky's theories and my appropriation of them assumes, as do some psychological understandings of color, that color speaks universally. Just because color in the Bible is symbolic for me, symbolic intent is not a given. However, I believe that on at least subconscious levels, color symbolism is real. It could also be that the biblical writers said more than they intended or knew. Yet my intuitive sense is that biblical authors used color to express qualities they associated with God and successfully communicated their sightings across the centuries.

Liturgical colors used in Roman Catholic, Orthodox, and some mainline Protestant churches seem to support my thoughts that color has some universal connotations and conveys knowledge of God. Green stands for

2. Tillich, *Dynamics of Faith,* 42–3.

3. Kandinsky, *Concerning the Spiritual in Art,* xiv–v.

4. Ibid., 29.

hope. White is for purity. Violet symbolizes penance and mourning. Red, the color of fire, celebrates Pentecost, the birthday of the Church. Color teaches and carries faith.

On the other hand, feelings about color must sometimes be culturally conditioned. In China people wear white to funerals. Americans find black or darker colors to be appropriate expressions of sadness. Thus it seems best to me to consider color as a common language but not absolutely universal in meaning.

Three important colors in the Bible are blue, red, and green. Red and green together are important, as is the combination of blue and red.

BLUE

Blue in the Bible suggests God's purity and purifying presence. Kandinsky described blue as a "heavenly color."[5] His writings confirm my exact same thought that with blue we experience "a call to the infinite." He said blue evokes in us a desire for purity and transcendence.[6] Sapphire blue (sometimes translated as lapis lazuli), as a symbol of transcendence, is part of the Elders' vision in Exodus 24.

Perhaps because my feelings for blue were repressed, my conviction of the importance of blue in Exodus erupted with the swiftness and intensity of a conversion experience. One self-assigned project during my graduate school years compelled me to further investigate color in the Bible. During my first Old Testament class, taught by Professor John S. Kselman, SS, at Weston Jesuit School of Theology, I painted an abstract picture of God based on Exodus 24:9–18 where Moses and elders saw the God of Israel with a pavement of sapphire stones, "like the very heaven for clearness," under his feet. Clear can mean transparent. However, another meaning for artists is non-muddy color. At this time I discovered Russian watercolors in an art supply store in Cambridge. *Russian blue* is the purest blue I have ever seen. It is so clear that cobalt blue looks muddy in comparison.

Then when Moses went up the mountain, the glory of the Lord was like a devouring fire. My collage titled *God* suggests pure blue as foundation, context, and purifying presence. I painted Russian blue, cobalt, and ultramarine through tissue paper and then pasted bits of colored tissue onto the paper. In my mind's eye I saw every blurb before dabbing and

5. Ibid., 38.

6. Overy, *Kandinsky: The Language of the Eye*, 93.

pasting. A red dot symbolizes the glory of God. It seems to me that the experience of purifying blue prepared Moses to see the glory of God in fiery red. In what may have been a similar aesthetic experience of blue, Kandinsky painted *The Blue Mountain* (oil) in 1908 and 1909, and some have detected a biblical influence, if only apparent in the title.[7]

God's glory and purifying presence is conveyed through color and form in Ezekiel. Again, blue and red suggest the combination of purity and glory. In a description of God that is similar to the Exodus theophany, the writer of Ezekiel tells us, "And above the dome over their heads there was something like a throne, in appearance like sapphire; and seated above the likeness of a throne there was something that seemed like a human form" (Ezek 1:26). The writer goes on to describe the form as like fire, which implies some red in the flames with the splendor of the rainbow all around. "This was the appearance of the likeness of the glory of the LORD" (Ezek 1:28).

In his book, *The Language and Imagery of the Bible,* biblical scholar G. B. Caird said that the greater proportion of biblical language that refers to God is anthropomorphic. [8] He went on to say that while there are explicit denials that God has a body, he is envisioned as having one as in Isaiah 31:3. [9] However, he reminds us that in theophanies anthropomorphic language is used sparingly.[10] Because of the word *likeness,* Ezekiel's vision is not to be taken literally. The word *likeness* is also part of the accounts in Exodus of seeing God. Since abstraction guards against literalism, it seems especially appropriate to me to paint abstract pictures of God.

Sapphire blue is also symbolic of the best of humanity in contrast to people at their very worst. Because our best nature is an end, blue has teleological significance. In Lamentations blue participates in the beauty of humanity at our best. Slightly different translations of Lamentations 4:7 give nuances of meanings of blue as a symbol of humanity reaching toward goodness. The New Revised Standard Version states, "Her princes were purer than snow, whiter than milk; their bodies were more ruddy than coral, their hair like sapphire" (Lam 4:7). Instead of describing hair as sapphire, the Revised Standard Version states, ". . . the beauty of

7. Bellido, *Kandinsky,* 52.

8. Caird, *The Language and Imagery of the Bible,* 174.

9. Ibid., 175.

10. Ibid., 175.

their form was like sapphire." Hair connotes crowning glory. Form suggests eternal essence. In both cases, it seems to me that blue is connected with the best in humanity. Zion's children changed. Their faces became blacker than soot. Sapphire blue provides high contrast between human purity and sooty depravity described in the most horrific verses in the Old Testament where mothers eat their own children.

Blue is symbolic in the beginning of creation as well as end-time wholeness. In Ezekiel 28:13, sapphires are some of the stones mentioned as having been part of the Garden of Eden. Sapphire stones are also part of the foundation of the Heavenly City of Revelation 21. Thus blue is part of the restored Eden, the Heavenly City that is the destination of salvation history. Blue was present in Eden. Blue will again be present at the omega point when God wipes away every tear.

Before painting my first biblical abstract of God based on Exodus 24, I basked for several summers in the beauty of blue morning glories. Absorbing pure blue was like seeing the face of God as I did in the cobalt vases many years ago. Biblical study and aesthetic contemplation were the raw ingredients for the following poem.

Blue Sonnet

Blue morning glories reach from ground to sky,
Jacob's ladder connecting earth, heaven.
Singing angel muse patiently stands by.
Pure hue, glory loveliness is leaven.
Hagar looking upon the face of God
Lived. So shall those whose gaze is strong enough
To embrace the icon nourished in sod.
Beauty so deep sadness is joyful hush.
Fathers of Israel saw beneath God's feet
A sapphire pavement. Hallow, praise, chant.
Sing in Heaven's City evil's defeat.
Foundations of treasured, precious blue stone,
Power, purest presence, God's face alone.

RED

Kandinsky assessed red as having powerful intensity. "The glow of red is within itself," he wrote in *Concerning the Spiritual in Art.*[11] In scripture red is sometimes implied rather than directly stated. Red makes an ontologi-

11. Kadinsky, *Concerning the Spiritual in Art*, 40.

cal statement because red reveals God's strength and power that back up God's word. One of the most familiar stories of the Old Testament is the story of Moses and the burning bush that must have been fiery red. Moses tended his father-in-law's flocks. He came to Mount Horeb, the mountain of God. Moses did not realize that he saw a messenger of Yahweh until he heard a divine voice from the burning bush. God spoke out of the burning bush of fiery red color saying, *"I am who I am."*

A shadow reflection of God gives high contrast to the fiery glory of God in Exodus 33. The Lord told Moses that he would do the very things that Moses requested. Moses said, "'Show me your glory, I pray'" (Exod 33:18). The Lord told Moses to stand on a rock while his glory passed by. God would put Moses in the cleft of a rock and cover Moses's face with his hand until divine glory passed. Then God would remove his hand and Moses would see God's back. "But my face shall not be seen" (Exod 33:23).

I painted Exodus 33:17–23 at the requests of Professors Leander E. Keck and Christopher R. Seitz during a biblical studies course at Yale Divinity School. One night before falling asleep, I pondered how to paint the backside of God. On Good Friday morning I woke up with an analogy, "The backside of God is to Exodus 33:23 what shadow is to Hebrews 8:5." In my painting, "Presence in Shadow: God in Exodus 33" I depicted God in a glorious red-orange swirling cloud floating by with a purple-gray shadow on the ground. Shadows do not mean absence because shadows are connected to people or things. God's backside is shadowed presence.

As a symbol, red participates in Jesus's divine nature and repeats the ontological statement of God's being in Exodus. When evening came, Jesus was on the land. The disciples were out in the boat. Then early in the morning the disciples had to row against an adverse wind. "When he saw that they were straining at the oars against an adverse wind, he came to them early in the morning walking on the sea" (Mark 6:48). The disciples were terrified, thinking that Jesus was a ghost. Mark wrote of Jesus's assurance. "'Take heart, it is I; do not be afraid'" (Mark 6:50). The words *"it is I"* echo *"I am who I am."* Jesus by implication shares in God's being.

This story builds upon the story in chapter 4 of Jesus stilling a storm with the strength of a divine harbormaster. Jesus had power over storm and chaos. Thus the story of Jesus walking on the water adds conviction of Jesus's divine essence to the statement of Jesus's power and authority. It takes only a little imagination to envision the scene of Jesus walking across the sea toward the disciples with a red sky in the background. A gathering morning storm suggests the old saying that children from coastal New England learn early in life: "Red sky in the evening, sailors delight. Red sky in the morning, sailors take warning." An account in Matthew suggests that this observation of the red morning sky was also part of the ancient world. In addressing the Pharisees' need for a sign, Jesus said that the Pharisees would say that there would be fair weather if in the evening the sky was red. If the morning sky was red they would say the weather would be stormy (Matt 16:2–3). A red sky in the background, even though it is not explicitly mentioned, could be in Kandinsky's terms the outer form of the biblical writer's inner conviction of Jesus's strength. Red in the background backs up Jesus's power and being.

Red is the color of Pentecost, the birthday of the church. Followers of Jesus sat in their house church. "Divided tongues, as of fire, appeared among them, and a tongue rested on each of them" (Acts 2:3). All were filled with the Holy Spirit. Red fills the human spirit with courage and strength.

GREEN

Green is the color of nourishment, refreshment, vitality, and fruitfulness. Many biblical references to green create textured, thick impasto color. Green vegetation needs water and moisture. It is not surprising that in dry biblical lands where lack of moisture can mean death green is associated with life-giving attitudes and productivity.

In Genesis 1:30 and 9:3 green plants for food are gifts from the Creator. Genesis 18 tells us the story of Abraham, Sarah, and the three visitors. The Lord appeared to Abraham by the oaks of Mamre. Three men were with the Lord. Sarah prepared a meal for the guests, who told her and Abraham that Sarah would have a child. It is easy to visualize oak trees with green leaves and associate green with the new life of a baby.

Artists can do exegesis, interpretation, and visual exhortation through color. A mosaic in San Vitale, Ravenna, called "The Feast of Abraham and the Three Men,"[12] depicts the warm, green world of the Old Testament. The leaves on the oak tree are hunter and sage green. Moss on the tree trunks repeats the green of the leaves. The background hills are peridot. Some Christians have interpreted the three men who visited Abraham by the oaks of Mamre in Genesis 18 as a preview of the Trinity. It is just as

12. Snyder, *Medieval Art,* color plate 16, 140.

plausible, it seems to me, to see the green in Genesis as a visual foreshadowing of the green in Mark's gospel.

In Psalm 23 the psalmist assures us that we shall find green pastures of rest. Kandinsky's writings describe green as the most restful color.[13] Rest is important for ongoing flowering and flourishing. In Psalm 92 the righteous flourish like the palm tree. Speaking of righteous people, the psalmist declared, "In old age they still produce fruit; they are always green and full of sap . . ." (Ps 92:14).

Psalm 52 and Proverbs 11 associate the color green with trust and flourishing. The psalmist understood that trust keeps alive the ability to be thankful. "But I am like a green olive tree in the house of God. I trust in the steadfast love of God forever and ever. I will thank you forever, because of what you have done" (Ps 52:8–9). The more didactic writer of Proverbs gives a snappy summary: "Those who trust in their riches will wither, but the righteous will flourish like green leaves" (Prov 11:28).

Jeremiah 17 connects the vitality of staying green with trust and faithfulness. The prophet adds a note of blessedness that perhaps anticipated the beatitudes because the blessed shall become like a tree planted by water. There is anticipation of future fulfillment as there is in the beatitudes. Thus the color green has an eschatological dimension. "Blessed are those who trust in the LORD, whose trust is the LORD. They shall be like a tree planted by water, sending out its roots by the stream. It shall not fear when heat comes, and its leaves shall stay green; in the year of drought it is not anxious, and it does not cease to bear fruit" (Jer 17:7–8). A tree of life connotes ongoing growing and giving. Trusting in God keeps fear at bay and life fruitful. The tree in Jeremiah also suggests the tree of life in Proverbs 3 that is associated with wisdom as an ingredient of happiness. "She is a tree of life to those who lay hold of her; those who hold her fast are called happy" (Prov 3.18).

In the New Testament the color green also has significance for the future. Green by implication participates in the announcement of the coming kingdom of God. Mark loved green and growing things. In Mark's parable a seed spouts by a mysterious process, like the coming reign of God (Mark 4:26–29).

In Mark 6, in the story of the feeding of five thousand people, Jesus orders the people to sit down in groups on the green grass. The color of

13. Overy, *Kandinsky, the Language of the Eye*, 93.

the grass is not mentioned in parallel accounts in Matthew and Luke. The writer of John does not tell us the color of the grass, but he makes a little more of the grass by saying, "There was a great deal of grass in the place . . ." (John 6:10b). (I sometimes wonder if Mark and John share a farmer's information source!) I do think that Mark and John have a shared theological aesthetic. Strong contrasts in the powers of dark and light typify John's gospel. Similarly, Mark's gospel is somber. Sometimes the disciples with next to no faith in Mark seem like the people who live in darkness in John in contrast to the people who live in the light. In contrast to the darkness of doubt in Mark there is also happy green and glorious illuminating white. Mark was overwhelmed with the whiteness of Jesus's clothing in the Transfiguration. He was so touched that he could barely find the words. He said that Jesus's clothes became dazzling white such as no one on earth could bleach (Mark 9:3). Artists might reply, "That's titanium white."

Dazzling white and fresh green are eschatological hints of glory and new life that dawned in the kingdom and post-Easter experience. The New Testament Greek word for green connotes the fresh, wet, happy yellow-green of spring. In Mark's story, Jesus as Good Shepherd tends his flock. The gathered sit on the green grass. When Jesus and his disciples fed the five thousand, all the people ate and were filled. The New Testament Greek word for filled or satisfied originally meant with animal food.[14] The oblique hint here is that as hay-fed animals, green grass aesthetically nourished people gathered around Jesus. Mark was the most emotional gospel writer. My sense is that he associated green grass with plants for food in Genesis and with the pastures of rest in Psalm 23. As noted previously, church historian Roland Bainton provides insight about the role of emotional sensitivity. He said that Martin Luther verged on saying that emotional sensitivity is a mode of revelation.[15] Mark's emotional nature may have helped him see that green nourishes souls as fish and bread feed bodies. The voice of God comes through the color green. I believe that Kandinsky would have understood my argument. Light, juicy green made an impression on him when he was three years old. [16] He thought of art as spiritual bread.[17] Color is one ingredient in art that provides spiritual bread.

14. Zerwick and Grosvenor, *A Grammatical Analysis of the New Testament*, 124–5.

15. Bainton, *Here I Stand*, 283.

16. Whitford, *Watercolours and Other Works on Paper*, 209.

17. Ibid., 25.

Similarly my Puritan ancestor, Jonathan Edwards, said that when we are delighted with flowers, meadows, green trees, and fields, we should see them as emanations of the sweet benevolence of Jesus Christ.[18] The smiling face of Christ renews the heart for communion and service. My painting "Green" is composed of green free-form bands to remind me of the rich texture of many references to green in the Bible. My hope is that it invites restful contemplation that renews strength for living.

Hildegard of Bingen, a twelfth-century mystic, was another sensitive soul who understood that green has religious significance. She wrote of the creative conduct of all living creatures emerging from the green vitality of human volition. She spoke of God's perfect power as the greening power and believed that the Holy Spirit poured out green freshness into the hearts of men and women so that they might bear good fruit.[19] Biblical references to green support her thoughts, especially Psalm 92 that describes righteous old people as "always green and full of sap." Eight centuries after Hildegard praised greening vitality, May Sarton wrote her poem, "Summer Music" in which she said, "Summer is all a green sound . . ." [20]

The use of green and blue in the Bible is unique in the ancient world and may reflect an aesthetic ability to see colors and use them symbolically. Eleanor Irwin in her book, *Colour Terms in Greek Poetry,* said that red and yellow made more impact on the Greeks than blue and green, and she added that the Greeks were slow to describe the sky as blue and the grass as green. [21]Mark definitely refers to the green grass. The heavenly context of God throughout the Bible is sapphire or lapis (an alternate translation) blue. Connecting green with nourishing, life-giving moisture and blue with a transcendent, purifying presence is a religious and aesthetic attainment.

Green and red are used together in *Revelation* to subtly suggest that God has both masculine and feminine qualities. In his book *The Bible as History: A Confirmation of the Book of Books* Werner Keller said that in ancient Israel red and blue were colors for men's clothing. Green seems to have been reserved for women.[22] In the context of heavenly worship, John

18. Sherry, *Spirit and Beauty,* 14.
19. Fox, *Hildegard of Bingen's Book of Divine Works,* 225.
20. Daziel, *Sarton Selected,* 124.
21. Irwin, *Colour Terms in Greek Poetry,* 201–2.
22. Keller, *The Bible as History,* 217.

of Patmos wrote: "At once I was in the spirit, and there in heaven stood a throne, with one seated on the throne! And the one seated there looks like jasper and carnelian, and around the throne is a rainbow that looks like an emerald" (Rev 4:2–3). Jasper is brown-red quartz. Carnelian is also reddish quartz. Kandinsky helps us appreciate what happens when red has a touch of brown in it. He said that when brown is added, vermilion rings like a great trumpet. As we have seen, red connotes strength and power. Green is the color of refreshment. Through carnelian God speaks with the power of a trumpet. Red matches God's paternal yet also maternal power to assess and save. Green coordinates with God's maternal yet also paternal nature to nurture and renew.

Kandinsky believed that the harmony of red and green is beautiful. [23] My painterly New Testament abstract, "God in Revelation," depicts God in brown-red surrounded by emerald green rainbow bands. There is beauty in a harmonious vision of God as both father and mother as well as having both masculine and feminine attributes as we all do in various blends because people are unique yet made in God's image. The use of red and green to suggest both masculine and feminine attributes in God might be an unintended feminist statement, hidden in the subconscious minds of patriarchal biblical writers. Intended or not, the use of color in *Revelation* is a first-century subversion of patriarchy. The thrust of this nonverbal challenge to understanding God as exclusively masculine is an invitation to re-read and re-interpret biblical texts with the assurance that God is beyond all words.

23. Kandinsky, *Concerning the Spiritual in Art*, 40.

9

Imagining God's Love with St. Ignatius of Loyola

During the beginning of the course in Ignatian spirituality, my late Rockport neighbor, Pat, who is missed by all who knew her, asked, "What are you doing today? Reading in your book?" The book she had in mind is *Ignatius of Loyola: The Psychology of a Saint.* I replied that I had a chipmunk story in the word processor. That story *Chipmunks' Christmas Cabin* was my way of integrating new learning from Saint Ignatius. Fr. Brian O. McDermott, SJ, did not ask to keep my A- paper from that class, but he did ask to keep *Chipmunks' Christmas Cabin.* That says something. *Chipmunks' Christmas Cabin* is a story of Ignatian discernment through quiet, prayerful attention to inner movements of thought. I fancy that St. Ignatius, also, appreciates my chipmunk tales. In *Biblical Theology and the Spiritual Exercises,* Gilles Cusson, SJ, said that any small creature could put Ignatius in contact with God. He perceived that "nothing exists or subsists without the active and loving presence of God; and that in return every creature becomes, in its own way, a reflection and proclamation of the divine grandeur."[1] At home we cast modesty aside and refer to my characters as Ignatian chipmunks! In my sense of things, imagination is one facet of human sensitivities that is a mode or revelation. I access latent faith and articulate belief through writing poetry and fiction.

How then does imagination reveal God? By imagination I do not mean completely made up or fictitious. Rather, imagination that is revelatory comes from openness to the power of sacred scriptures, art, the humanities as God's helper to keep us human, and beauty to engage our minds and hearts to imagine and sometimes image or picture God.

Experiences may also be a bridge to God. In his book, *Ignatius of Loyola: The Psychology of a Saint,* W. W. Meissner, SJ, MD, explains the con-

1. Cusson, *Biblical Theology and the Spiritual Exercises*, 321.

cept of a transitional bridge. The basic idea is that the transitional experience straddles subjective and objective realms of experience. "Reading a poem or immersing oneself in music or painting, for example, takes place in the intermediate realm of illusion, in which the esthetic experience is neither subjective nor objective but something of both."[2]

When I wrote the chipmunk stories in this chapter as a way of integrating the course, "The Theological and Pastoral Dimensions of *The Spiritual Exercises of St. Ignatius (of) Loyola*," I was clearly in a subjective realm. If God exists, then I was also on a bridge between the subjective and objective reality of God. Of course, God's existence is open to debate, but since the main idea of this book is that there are hints that God does exist, I do fault to the side of proceeding as if there is an objective truth. However, cultural conditioning suggests images of God or the ways in which we imagine and picture transcendence. Thus my notions of objective truth are provisional.

Embracing beautiful images of transcendent good will in literature, art, or nature can be, I believe, a transitional experience or a bridge to God. Social experience, such as fellowship, is also a bridge. Beauty in nature, the convictions of intuition and imagination, and a sense of completion in community are all matrixes in which to feel assurance of love. Of course, a continuing concern is wondering if insights and images of beauty or transcendent good will or God's love that are experienced on that transitional bridge correspond to something real. Maybe not, yet maybe yes. Imagination may clear away the briars in the mind to make a path to felt knowledge.

Ignatius of Loyola wrote a spiritual masterpiece now called *The Spiritual Exercises of St. Ignatius, Loyola* (hereafter *The Spiritual Exercises*). Imaginative immersion in this prayer process may be a bridge between people and the divine. Long before he became a saint, Ignatius of Loyola used both imagination and intellect to help himself and other people discover things about themselves and their relationship to Christ. I base the following summary on the first course I took at Weston, "The Theological and Pastoral Dimensions of *The Spiritual Exercises of St. Ignatius Loyola*," and Meissner's book.

Saint Ignatius of Loyola was a-sixteenth century warrior converted to pilgrim seeker who founded the Jesuits in 1540. He was born around 1491 and named Inigo at birth. Shortly after his birth, his mother died. A

2. Meissner, *Ignatius of Loyola*, 389–90.

devout woman, Maria, taught Inigo his first prayers and nursed him. Like his famed contemporary, Christopher Columbus, Ignatius was an adventurer, not on the ocean, but on the sea of spiritual ebb and flow. He was contentious and Catholic, chivalrous and charming. Eventually he would convert to deeper reverence. After wild adventures on the sea of high living, he became a soldier and found military discipline fitting. He pushed on when others would have stopped and was severely wounded in the leg during the battle of Pamplona. Defining himself as the indomitable soldier was no longer possible. Eventually he would sight solid ground and write that the true destiny of humanity is to "praise, reverence, and serve God." The journey from worldly warrior to finding company with Jesus was conversion of heart, mind, and soul.

While recovering from his wounds in the family castle, Inigo read books about Christ and the lives of saints because the popular chivalrous novels were not available. Fantasy about heroic deeds shifted to thinking about all he could do as a soldier of Christ.

In time Inigo studied and received the name *Ignatius* with his master's degree. Saint Ignatius, who himself lost his mother as an infant, developed a maternal bearing toward his students. His religious masterpiece, *The Spiritual Exercises*, is a metaphorical boat-building manual designed to launch people into deeper spiritual waters. These prayer processes have over the centuries helped people become closer to Christ and also discern their callings through engaging, imaginative exercises based on the life of Christ.

In the exercise, "Contemplation to Obtain Love," he wrote, "I will consider how God labors and works for me in all the creatures on the face of the earth; that is, he acts in the manner of one who is laboring. For example, he is working in the heavens, elements, plants, fruits, cattle, and all the rest—giving them their existence, conserving them, concurring with their vegetative and sensitive activities, and so forth. Then I will reflect on myself."[3]

The words "concurring with their sensitive activities" suggest to me the idea that God takes our tendencies and sensitivities and works with them. The thought that God is working for us in the elements, plants, and heavens can mean that God nourishes our souls through these things.

3. Ganss, *The Spiritual Exercises of Saint Ignatius Loyola*, 95.

Eventually I wrote four more chipmunk stories. In *Sandy's Special Gift*, Sandy finds his way to be like the Great Sunflower in a way analogous to how Christians try to imitate Christ. Yes, it is lightly veiled autobiography from my New Hampshire days about tutoring children who had learning disabilities. One second grade girl, Barbara, had coordination difficulties much like mine. In some ways I am preaching to myself. *Big Mistake* makes it clear that bad choices have consequences. *County Fair* combines Exodus deliverance and Easter joy realized in the present moment. Biblical scholars might call it a story of realized eschatology or a taste, in Paul Tillich's words, of the "eternal now." In this story grace is the experience of tasting the sweetness with the joy remaining in the heart. *Sunflower Days* is a story of God's abiding presence and steadfast love. Perhaps some readers will like to read these stories to their children or grandchildren.

CHIPMUNKS' CHRISTMAS CABIN

Two weeks before Christmas, the year Sarah was five, Sarah and Mother made a gingerbread house. The nut-brown house had a snow-covered roof made of frosting, rounded windows, and a door with red licorice hinges that looked just like leather. Sarah and Mother decorated that fancy Victorian home with red and white candy canes, peppermint swirls, and pale pink wintergreen candies.

Mother and Sarah put the Victorian gingerbread house on the table in front of the window. They added pretend fluffy snow and a collection of wooden people dressed in Christmas red. Mother remembered the cabin house she and Sarah had made the previous year. Since no one could bear to throw away the gingerbread log cabin, Mother wrapped it in tissue paper and stored it in an old trunk in the attic. "Remember the house we made last year?" she asked. Sarah remembered all the details—the fat chimney on top, the logs trimmed in white, the first little door with red hinges and the square windows. Mother added, "We cannot keep every house. It is time to put the old one out in the yard. Perhaps some animal will find a use for it."

So Sarah and Mother took last year's gingerbread cabin out into the backyard and put it in front of the rock pile, which Father built. "Never know when you could use some more rocks," he often said. Everyone knew the rock pile would stay in place for years, because there already was a stone wall around the front yard, the backyard, the vegetable garden, the flower garden, and the doghouse!

The winter air was very cold. The gingerbread cabin froze immediately. Even Onyx the crow would not be able to break it apart with his beak and eat it.

One day when the sun ever so slightly warmed the rock pile, Mr. and Mrs. Chipmunk came out of their hole in the rock pile. They spotted the gingerbread cabin. "What a lovely home," said Mrs. Chippie, as she was affectionately nicknamed in the neighborhood. Mr. Chippie agreed and offered to help move in right away. The wind had blown a pile of leaves on the backside of the rock pile where there were no snowdrifts. On moving day it was easy to bring leaves for making warm beds into the house. The door with the red hinges was open in welcome.

When winter started to bend toward spring, four babies were born to Mr. and Mrs. Chippie. They slept and ate and ate and slept until they were big enough to venture outside to play. The air became warmer but not hot enough to melt the ice on the rock ledge above the cabin.

Then as the days grew still lighter and warmer, the ice began to melt.

Drip, drip, and drip. The melting ice fell onto the chipmunks' Christmas cabin. After four days of thaw, the home collapsed. The little chipmunks were frightened and sad. Mother chipmunk was very quiet and then said, "Our winter cabin was good fortune. However our old home, the one we had before you little ones were born, will be a cooler summer home. Maybe next year another house will come along. The human people who live in the big house do many of the same things year after year. Every year when the days are darkest, they put lights on the bushes outside. Then they throw popcorn and dried cranberries onto the ground. When the days are brighter, they hide colored eggs in the grass. Perhaps in time they will put out more houses."

Then Father chipmunk, who had been inspecting the ruins, discovered that the water had turned the cabin into peppermint, gingerbread pudding!

"Party time," said Mother Chippie. "We do not have company very often since chipmunks are not very sociable. Yet, with thankful hearts, we must share this unexpected gift of Christmas pudding. We have an abundance of stored ragweed seeds also."

The chipmunk family sent out their call to all the other chipmunks, who lived in nearby stone walls. Soon there was a large happy gathering. The celebration began. Mother chipmunk noticed two gray squirrels looking lovingly at the treat. She had meant to become better acquainted with the squirrel neighbors but had just not gotten around to it. So the squirrels were invited to the feast, which was a surprise even to the Chippies themselves.

Sarah and Mother continued the tradition of making a gingerbread house every year. Each December they put the old one outside. Generation after generation of chipmunks found a new winter home, house after house, after house, after house.

Bible verse: "'Behold, I make all things new'" (Rev 21:5 RSV).

Prayer: Dear God, when things go wrong help us to use our heads to think and our hearts to trust. Amen.

SANDY'S SPECIAL GIFT

Sandy Chipmunk was very sad. He had downcast eyes that showed hurt inside his heart.

Sandy was different from the other young chipmunks. Most chipmunks have a touch of red in their fur. Sandy had red spots. Sandy liked his name because his name suggested that red hair is nice. However, he did not like to be called *Measles*. Just hearing that name made him feel feverish inside. "Never mind," said his mother. "Chipmunks are sometimes unthinking but never really unkind. Someday others will appreciate you. Sometime you will find your special talent that you can share. So yearn for light and love from above. Take time to notice when you feel close to the Great Sunflower in the sky."

Sandy listened to his mother. Still, *someday* and *sometime* felt far away. To make matters worse, Sandy ran with his tail up. Eastern chipmunks run with their tails out straight. Sometimes Sandy's friends teased him, saying, "Only chipmunks west of the Mississippi," and they always spelled it out, *M-I-S-S-I-S-S-I-P-P-I*, "keep their tails up. Where did you come from? Certainly not from around here!"

Sandy could not even go on trips to gather ragweed seeds because ragweed made him sneeze. Worst of all, Sandy felt that he did not have a way to be like the Great Sunflower in the sky or to imitate the sunflowers that spring from the earth. For chipmunks offer their gifts of friendship by being in some small way something like the sunflowers of the earth and the Great Sunflower, the sun in the sky.

Father Chipmunk was dependable like the sun that day after day rises and sets.

Mother Chipmunk, like the sunflowers in the garden that give nourishing seeds, provided food for her family. Young chipmunks gathered ragweed seeds. Then they frolicked and played like dancing sunbeams on the stone walls.

Mother Chippie often reminded Sandy that someday he would find his special gift to give. And so it was. One night in late winter the chipmunks gathered in family circles to think about ways to celebrate the return of spring. Mother Chippie said she would gather violet seeds in her mouth pouch and take them to the ant colony in the dry patch of the garden. "Ants do enjoy violet seeds and welcome all gifts of neighborliness."

Father Chippie said he would offer his strength to help other chipmunks have a better life. "Not all chipmunks are strong enough to dig deep, safe paths. I can make more tunnels so that all chipmunks can travel safely."

Sandy's sister and two brothers said they would teach their lively games and dances to all the baby chipmunks to soon be born.

"Sandy, how do you want to give warmth and friendship like the Great Sunflower? How can you be a little sunflower?

Sandy was very quiet for a moment and then he spoke. "I am good company and a good friend to other little critters who do not do things that other creatures do well. I have never thought of my ways of playing as a gift before, but play is a gift to me that I share. Bethany the little bunny who hurt her left leg cannot play bunny hop with her brothers and sisters. You know how baby bunnies hop over each other early in the morning when the grass is covered with dew. Bethany learns hopping by hopping over me. We have fun playing.

"One day Tom the toad who has lost one eye played with me in the peppermint patch and we found him a safe hiding place. A flowerpot was hidden among the tall, leafy peppermint plants. I asked the squirrels to help dig a hole underneath it for an entrance so Tom Toad would have a house to shelter him from the sun. They even nibbled out a little above-the-ground door.

"Ever since the squirrels came to our Christmas party they have been more willing to take a break from acorn gathering to play with me and help other animals. All the squirrels have become good company. Together we will care and share.

"Grandmother Mouse worries about the little grand-mice. I listen to her and then tell the little ones about ways to be safe and remind them that their Grandmother Mouse loves them with all her heart."

Suddenly Sandy felt his heart warm. He felt close to the Great Sunflower. Sandy smiled.

Bible verse: "Let your light shine . . ." (Matt 5:16 NRSV).

Prayer: Dear God, please help us find our gifts to share. Amen.

BIG MISTAKE

"No, you may not go to the Cherry Hill Farm tonight," said Mother Chippie to her two chipmunk sons and their friend, the son of the chipmunks who live near the ferns. "There are rules. Like it or not, there are just some things that grown-up chipmunks can do that younger chipmunks cannot. Going to the farm to sip cherry wine that comes from fermenting cherries that fall into the water in rock basins is one of things you may not do."

Now the three chipmunks, who were nicknamed *Button, Mutton,* and *Peanut,* were angry. Besides, they disliked their nicknames. Almost everyone had forgotten their real names, Thaddeus, Theodore, and Nathaniel. Button's name came from his cute nose, which his mother said looked just like a little black button. She chose Mutton for his brother's name because it rhymed with Button and Mutton at birth was as cuddly as a lamb. The chipmunks that lived in the ferns chose the name Peanut for their son because Peanut's father thought peanuts are the most special treat.

When Mrs. Chippie went back to her work in the back burrow where she could not hear, Mutton spoke. "We are too old for these names, and we can prove it. Tonight we will sneak out and go to the farm. Nothing can hurt us. Farmers don't drive their tractors at night. The only cat on the farm is that old, black-and-white cat named Yin-Yang. He just sits around meditating all day. He always obeys his owner. Every morning she tells him, "Don't you ever bring me a chipmunk. Moles are okay to catch but never chipmunks."

So on the darkest of nights, the three chipmunks put chestnuts and feathers into their beds to look like sleeping chipmunks and sneaked out of their burrow homes. The path through the briars was well-worn and easy to travel. Hawks could not see through the thickets. "This is easy," said Button. Mutton and Peanut agreed.

Soon the chipmunk trio came to the barn. The rock basins filled with wine were in back of the barn only a short distance from a garden of gourds. "What fun," said Mutton. "We can drink wine and then climb on the gourds. We could hollow one out with our teeth to make it into a boat. Sailing in the drinking trough will be a real blast."

Button, Mutton, and Peanut sipped a little wine; then they sipped some more. Mutton sang a song, and Button became very silly singing, "Button is my name. Cussing is my game." Peanut began to look worried and thought, *Maybe Button and Mutton will stop sipping if we go for a boat ride.* So he talked the others into launching a gourd boat from the pile of seed bags near the trough.

At first paddling around in their yellow-and-green gourd boat was fun. But then Button and Mutton became rowdy, pushing and shouting. They stood up in the boat. Suddenly Button fell overboard.

Peanut, who had sipped very little, said, "Mutton, stay to the left to balance the boat." Then he reached out his right arm to Button and told him to hang on until they could reach the end of the trough where Button could climb onto the seed bags. As soon as all the chipmunks had climbed onto the seed bags and rowed toward shore, Button fell off into the mud. He laughed and laughed and rolled around while Mutton and Peanut wondered what to do. Then out of the corner of his eye, Mutton spied the old cat. "Watch out," he cried. "Yin-Yang is out tonight." Button just laughed some more and said, "You know Yin-Yang just chases moles. He never goes after chipmunks."

However, being an old cat, Yin-Yang did not see too well, even in the dark when cats see best. Furthermore, he was told that he could catch moles. Button, covered with mud and moving very slowly because he was quite drunk, looked just like a mole. The chase was on. Button was not lucky. The cat grabbed his tail in his mouth and bit about half of it off. Then he realized he had caught a chipmunk and stopped.

Button, Mutton, and Peanut slowly started toward home. They sneaked back into their beds. But in the morning Button had to explain to his father and mother why he had only half a tail. Father and Mother

Chippie were very quiet for a long time. Finally Father Chippie spoke. "Breaking the rules is not a good way to live. If you had waited until you were older to visit the farm, you would not likely have drunk too much and fallen overboard. You must think about the best ways to live life. And going through life with only half a tail will not be easy."

Button was indeed sorry. He cried. He knew his actions made the Great Sunflower sad. Mutton and Peanut were also sorry for their mistakes.

Mr. and Mrs. Chippie and the chipmunks of the ferns arranged for their sons to spend some time apart in the peace and beauty of a moss garden. The chipmunk parents told Button, Mutton, and Peanut that after they had given serious thought about the best ways to live, they would be called by their real names, Thaddeus, Theodore, and Nathaniel or the friendly, grown-up nicknames, Thad, Ted, and Nat. For after all, among true friends and family, nicknames can be reminders of love.

Bible Verse: "O give thanks to the LORD, for he is good; his steadfast love endures forever!" (Ps 118:1).

Prayer: Gracious God, help us to make good choices and believe in your steadfast love even when we make mistakes. Amen.

COUNTY FAIR

County fair. Just hearing those two words fill chipmunks with gladness. Their little black eyes sparkle with excitement. All summer young and old chipmunks look forward to fun and food. For little chipmunks the county fair is the best day of the year.

Often chipmunks like to play alone. Yet on the day of the fair several chipmunk families gathered in front of the stone wall. Wanting to look out for one another and be good company, they planned to scamper together to the fair grounds.

"We must watch out for cats and stay out of the road," said Father Chippie. "Keep as close as you can to the stone walls and fences." The chipmunks set out on their journey. The sky was blue with white, fluffy clouds. Green leaves made soft rippling noises in the gentle breeze. Fields of happy, wet, yellow-green grass shimmered in the morning dew.

Single file, one by one, the chipmunks paraded along the top of a stone wall, past the blue morning glories that matched the sky and yellow daises with centers like chocolate drops.

At the end of the stone wall the chipmunks came to an open field. Father Chipmunk, taking the lead, said, "Now it is time to follow the fence." So the chipmunks climbed down from the wall. Then, in horror, they saw that the motionless black form on the ground was not the shadow of the fencepost but Panther, the young, fast, black yet partially blind cat. "Use your wits," said Father Chippie at a pitch that Panther could not hear. "I will try to distract him while you run to the next stone wall."

Father Chippie switched his tail back and forth on the ground to get Panther's attention. The other chipmunks ran as fast as they could across the open field. Alas, Panther did not seem as interested in chasing Father Chippie as he was in catching Sandy, the chipmunk that moved quite slowly. The chase was on. The sun was bright. Cats, especially those who do not see very well, see better in the dark. So Panther went on instinct and reached out to grab Sandy by the tail. Since Sandy ran with his tail up, unlike the other chipmunks, Panther took hold of a tree root he mistook for Sandy's tail. Assuming that all chipmunks are alike was Panther's mistake.

Then a most amazing thing happened. The breezes ruffled the leaves, letting sunlight shine directly on Panther's face. For a moment he could not see at all. Several green, hard acorns fell on Panther's head. His head stung. Unable to move, he stopped just long enough for all the chipmunks to find safe hiding places. Panther's pride was hurt. He could not catch even the slowest chipmunk. He went home with his head hung low and his tail dragging on the ground.

Safe in the stone wall, the chipmunks rested in silence. Father Chippie said, "We must pause and give thanks to the Great Sunflower in the sky for blinding Panther long enough for us to escape. We must remember and tell our children, who will tell their children, of the day when the Great Sunflower parted the leaves and caused acorns to fall on our enemy. We must also remember that not all chipmunks always escape from cats. We are not better than those who are lost." After the chipmunks offered thanks, they drank water from the little cup in the crevice of a rock and shared seeds from the pinecones on the ground.

With renewed spirits, the chipmunks marched to the fairgrounds. Mother Chippie spotted the perfect place to camp for the day. The picnic area was safe. People did not park their cars there. An apple tree gave shade as well as little green apples. There were many hiding places in logs and leaves. Best of all, people never brought cats on their picnics.

What a day it was! A band played happy music. The sky had never looked so blue or the grass so green. Human families gathered around the picnic tables. Friendly children shared their treats with the chipmunks. Children and chipmunks enjoyed pieces of hot dog rolls, popcorn, pretzels, bagels, potato chips, and cheese crackers.

Late in the afternoon, families began to pack up and leave. Just as the chipmunks were ready to start back to their home, Mother spotted a huge ball of pink cotton candy on the ground. What a treat! "Wait!" she called. "We must decide whether we should eat it now or take it home. Do we save it and have a reminder of our pleasant day? Or do we taste and savor now? How do we honor the light and love in this happy day? The candy is covered with paper. We could easily drag it home. Should we?"

All the chipmunks pondered thoughtfully. Most wanted to eat the cotton candy right away but were not sure the others would agree. Finally Sandy spoke up, saying, "Life, as I found out today, is very precious. Sometimes the time to celebrate is the present moment. We can share and enjoy now."

Yes, agreed all the chipmunks. Very happy chipmunks nibbled until all the candy was gone. The youngest chipmunks were covered with pink, sweet sparkles of sugar.

Contented chipmunks started toward home. On the way a gentle rain fell. The chipmunks knew they had done the right thing. If they had taken the candy home, the rain would have washed it all away. Having tasted sweetness, the joy would stay in their hearts.

The soft rain tenderly washed the sticky little chipmunks. By the time they were home, the chipmunks were clean, sleepy, and ready for bed. Feeling very blessed, they quickly fell asleep while the stars in the sky twinkled.

Bible verse: "This is the day which the LORD has made; let us rejoice and be glad in it" (Ps 118:24).

Prayer: Dear God, please help us notice the happy times and be glad. Thank you. Amen.

SUNFLOWER DAYS

The sun, which chipmunks know as the Great Sunflower in the sky, shone on the sunflower shoots in the emerald green summer garden. Sunbeams warmed the soil and seedlings while working magic within every shoot. Sunlight labored inside each growing plant, which grew upward as if trying to touch the sun itself.

Then in the early days of fall, the trees cast dark shadows across the stone walls where the chipmunks play and build their underground burrows. The sunflowers started to nod their heads. They had done their work. Seeds in the heart of the sunflower blossoms were ripe and as black as the September shadows. During the winter months ahead, nourishing oils in the seed would give life to animals and birds. The sunflowers noticed all the good creatures in their garden and rested.

The black seeds and the darkest shadows of the year reminded the oldest chipmunks that warm days were almost over. Quiet retreats and winter naps would come soon.

Mother Chippie called her four young chipmunks together. She told them about the circle gathering in the garden patch. "Chipmunks gather to sing and dance among the sunflowers in this season of the sunflower sabbath. For we live in the presence of the Great Sunflower in the sky who knows our ways and understands all chipmunk desires.

"The golden petals of the sunflowers that spring from the earth are the last thing chipmunks notice and remember before our winter sleep. On the warmest winter afternoons the rays of the Great Sunflower gently awaken us. Each spring the face of the Great Sunflower smiles upon us with blessing. In return chipmunks offer gifts of song and dance."

On the day of the circle gathering, the chipmunk families met in the northeast corner of the garden where breezes from the ocean filled the air with salt perfume. Together they danced in twists and turns among all the flowers. They came together in the middle of the garden. Young chipmunks climbed upon tall, flat rocks in order to see the ceremony.

Each chipmunk, young or old, could speak when a spirit within rose up in a still, small voice, which named a blessing. And thus the chipmunks spoke of the treasures in their hearts. They testified to the loving spirit of the Great Sunflower, all shades of golden sunflower petals, the waxy scent of blue cedar berries, crimson sumac, which fills chipmunks with courage, plentiful crops of ragweed seeds, safe burrows, and wits to outsmart all cats.

The chipmunks joined their paw-hands. They lifted their heads upward to feel the sunlight on their faces and promised to remember summer warmth when winter nights are cold.

The chipmunks began to sway in their circle dance while singing with a rapping beat, "Swing to the left. Move to the right. Stand together. Hold on tight. Remember the promise of the sunflower days. Sunflower love will never depart. There will always be light working in our hearts."

Bible Verses: "I will sing of your steadfast love, O LORD, forever . . ." (Ps 89:1).

Prayer: Dear God, please help us keep our hearts open to your light and love. We sing and dance with joy.

Part 3

God's Actions

10

God Is, Cares, and Listens

Sometimes a person's least-favorite biblical book is the one that she or he most needs. So it was with me. I have always heeded Martin Luther's assessment of the New Testament book James. He saw it as an "epistle of straw."[1] Luther was deeply convinced that James was about salvation through work rather than through faith. Despite my reservations about the value of James, as far back as college I saw James as a counterbalance to the emphasis of justification by faith alone, which is a theme in Romans that many Protestants favor. Concluding that good works flow from faith and trust seems reasonable. Yet although I believed that faith and works are not mutually exclusive, my sense of counterbalance was not enough to allow me to emotionally believe in justification by faith or feel entitled to enjoy earthly rest in God. Calvinism filled my every pore. My feeling was, why make things worse by paying attention to James?

When writing my book *An Artistic Approach to New Testament Literature,* I had to reconsider James. My hermeneutic of suspicion turned into a hermeneutic of surprise. I discovered James's literary artistry, sound advice for Christian living, core claims about God that strengthen my beliefs, and spiritual company.

James is a New Testament book of great artistry. Possibly a biological brother of Jesus wrote it, but it is more likely that a spiritual brother who was very appreciative of tradition wrote it somewhere around 80–90 AD. It is best described as a wisdom instruction that is concerned with right behavior. This letter was written somewhere is the eastern Mediterranean world to a general audience that is so general that it seems contemporary and ecumenical.

1. Harrington, *Who is Jesus?* 159.

The artistic features of James's writing include texture, perspective, lovely line of thought, and a focal point that summarizes true religion. Texture comes from the author's use of the Old Testament. He explored and elaborated on the theme of love of neighbor, which is informed by Leviticus 19:18. This allusion to the Old Testament brings rich texture to James's writing. James's perspective is that getting along with others is important and that God-given wisdom bears the fruit of mercy. James's practical instructions, which give sound advice for Christian living, are like pearls of wisdom strung into a line necklace. Two of my favorite pearls are: 1. Words matter because they can both curse and bless (3:9–10), and 2. be a friend to God and God will be a friend to you (4:1–10). The focal point of James's wisdom instruction is like a golden clasp on a pearl necklace. "Religion that is pure and undefiled before God, the Father, is this: to care for orphans and widows in their distress, and to keep oneself unstained by the world" (Jas 1:27).

James affirms three claims about God. These convictions are that God is, God listens, and God cares, especially about the poor. Belief in God is a basic and profound belief. James wrote: "You believe that God is one; you do well" (2:19). James adds a personal dimension to belief in one God when he insists that God listens to the prayers of faithful people. "If any of you is lacking in wisdom, ask God, who gives to all generously and ungrudgingly, and it will be given you. But ask in faith, never doubting, for the one who doubts is like a wave of the sea, driven and tossed by the wind . . ." (1:5–6). This verse brings to mind the teaching of Jesus in Matthew 5:3 in which Jesus is a wise teacher. God-given wisdom was authoritative for James's community as it also was for Matthew's audience. God cares and is especially concerned about the poor. "Has not God chosen the poor in the world to be rich in faith and to be heirs of the kingdom that he has promised to those who love him?" (2:5). James's conviction of God's caring is the foundation for his definition of true religion that is the golden clasp of his necklace of wisdom teachings.

Finally James offers company in the ongoing task of putting beliefs into action. Protestants who have been raised in the social gospel tradition and Catholics who embrace liberation theology will find James conducive to their thinking. "Be doers of the word . . . " (1:22).

What, then, does James have to offer those of us, including myself, who are not physically strong and cannot be as active as other church members in strenuous physical work? We can be assured that we who are the more contemplative friends of God are also in God's company and find strength to keep on with our quieter, sometimes invisible forms of ministry. "Indeed we call blessed those who showed endurance. You have heard of the endurance of Job, and you have seen the purposes of the Lord, how the Lord is compassionate and merciful" (5:11). Of course, this consoling thought is widely applicable and speaks to muscular Christians as well as physically frail ones. Yet believing that all people who endure in various ways are blessed gives assurance that God cares. To believe in God's compassionate blessing is to grow in trust. With heightened trust it is more possible to believe in the implicit promise of inner peace, which brings a sense of rightness with God. Perhaps Martin Luther overlooked the promise in this verse.

11

God Welcomes

The Story of the Indigo Buntings

WELCOME INTO ETERNAL LIFE is a huge hint that there is a loving God. This story suggests that there is heavenly life for people who do not go to church and are not explicitly Christian. Lester, who was the best man at our wedding, asked if the following poem that we sent with our Christmas card in 2008 is true. Yes, it is.

INDIGO BUNTING SONNET

Two weeks before Eleanor Parsons died
I asked her for a sign from the Beyond
Specifying two indigo buntings
Loveliest birds, pure notes of heaven's song.
Two birds don't have to be in the same place.
Just one would seem like a coincidence.
Double sightings would make a stronger case,
Confirm God's wide welcome, love's deepest sense.
Before the memorial service day
A blessed sympathy note came in the mail
An indigo bunting: "Thank you." I prayed.
Bunting also on the back, my spirit sailed.
Proof or temporal ambiguity
Creating room for beauty's mystery?

Ellie, short for Eleanor, brought me up from the age of four after my first mother died. Her sister, Charlotte Hope (known as Hopie), who was egged on by her fundamentalist friend, told Ellie their concern that Ellie would not get to heaven because she was not a church member. Ellie did not know how much they insisted that I get a chaplain to have her join a church nearly on her deathbed. Although Ellie would not have put it this way, her sister's concerns gave her a bit of an existential crisis, which only assurance of her place in heaven could neatly address. Stanley M. Harrison in his introduction to *The Self as Agent* by John Macmurray discusses Macmurray's understanding that came early in his career of ultimate reality and authentic religion. Drawing from Macmurray's earlier essay, "Objectivity in Religion" (1927), Harrison says that Macmurray's central insight is simply stated. Harrison observes that desire for personal dimensions to ultimate reality is the context for Macmurray's philosophical search for reality. Harrison wrote, "The concern that people naturally have about the character of ultimate reality is rooted in the desire that ultimate reality be personal. If ultimately reality, God, isn't personal, then our deepest concerns as persons, symbolized by death, which threatens absolutely our existence in a personal world, can't finally be resolved."[1]

I ended up supporting Ellie and after her death put together an almost secular service. I remember how angry she was when as a teenager I wanted to join the Congregational Church and told me that I was just repeating things I had been told. That was not true. No one grows up or learns anything in a vacuum, but I have always thought for myself. Because my beliefs have not always been respected I know how important it is to respect the beliefs of other people. An explicitly Christian service would not have been reflective of Ellie and even worse a sign of vindictiveness. Yet telling the story, which Ellie would have loved, of the indigo bunting that I had not yet turned into a poem suggested assurance of God's broad love.

I do not know if Ellie substantially changed her religious beliefs toward the end of her life. I do know that the idea that people can change is a basic belief in Christianity. She did change her mind about me and no longer saw me as the shame of the family but as costar with Rosemary. Rosemary is my younger sister of heart and hearth. Ellie raised me with her after my first mother died. Rosemary is a Rockport harbormaster and also serves as an EMT. She is often featured in the local newspaper when she rescues people on land and sea. When people grow in understanding of one another it is easier, or so it seems to me, to envision the possibility of a world where there is good will that may reflect ultimate and transcen-

1. Macmurray, *The Self as Agent*, xi.

dent good will. Of course, there is room for mystery about the hearts of others and about the ways of God.

Gay Williams presided at the memorial service. She was a member of the First Congregational Church of Verona, New Jersey, when Ernie was a minister there. She moved to Massachusetts and after semi-retirement became a hospital chaplain. Without knowing that Ellie was my second mother, she visited her in the Addison Gilbert Hospital. Ellie had had a slight stroke and could not remember my last name but told Gay that she had two daughters, Rosemary and Sharon, who were very different but both very nice. "Rosemary is a harbormaster and Sharon is a poet." Gay, whom Ellie came to consider a third daughter, was the perfect person to conduct Ellie's service. I was very happy when one of Ellie's friends said that it was the service that she would have wanted.

So as the poem states, I asked Ellie for a sign and said that if she sent me two indigo buntings, I would write a poem about it and send a copy to Aunt Hopie and her friend. This request was a tall order. I have only seen two indigo buntings in my life. The first time I was eleven and spotted one in the backyard of our home in Pigeon Cove, which is the northern section of Rockport. Ellie asked how I knew the name of the bird. There was a tiny indigo bunting on the bottom of the page of the fifth-grade reader that I had the year before. The second spotting of an indigo bunting was in 1969 on the edge of the parking lot of an armory in New Hampshire where Ernie and I went to get our New Hampshire drivers' licenses.

Two indigo buntings came to me not as real birds but as photographs on a sympathy card from John and Betty, who live in Pigeon Cove. Betty told me there were different birds in the box of cards and she quickly picked one. Aunt Hopie was relieved by the poem. The flock of buntings grew. A few days after the memorial service, I found a card from my friend Ann with two indigo buntings. When I told the story to my friend Judy, she said she had a card with two indigo buntings and would send it to me. Her birds joined my collection.

Buntings as symbol took flight. While sorting through Ellie's books, Rosemary found a book entitled *The Indigo Bunting: A Memoir of Edna St. Vincent Millay* by Vincent Sheean. In the chapter with the same title as the book, the author shared some of Millay's last words that help me deal with grief through rejoicing in the color blue of many birds and varied shades and affirmation that there can be a perfect day. Therefore the color blue comforted me when my first mother died and also when my second mother died. Sheean wrote that Millay's sister Norma found Millay's notebooks with parts of a sonnet and then words marked "another poem."[2] I quote the couplets from the unfinished sonnet:

> Never before, perhaps, was such a sight—
> Only one sky (my breath!) and all that blue—
>
> Lapis, and Sèvres, and borage—every hue
> Of blue-jay—indigo bunting—bluebird's flight.[3]

The words marked "another poem" help me know that sometimes writers can write something that will matter even at the very end of life and that some days require grieving but not all. To echo Father James F. Keenan's definition of charity, Millay's words, like a loving mother, encourage me to keep writing poetry, which is the work that I love. Because Millay's poetic wisdom comes to me in a book that I inherited from Ellie, she also participates in that love. Millay wrote in her notes for another poem.

> I will control myself, or go inside.
> I will not flaw perfection with my grief.
> Handsome, this day: no matter who has died.[4]

Ellie, who was not at all comfortable with my interest in religion until the last year of her life, was not the person who I ever thought would help me address a theological problem. However, receiving the indigo buntings on the sympathy card strengthens the evidence for the existence of God and eternal life. Macmurray noted that there is both an agnostic and theistic wing to existentialism. He believed that "the theistic alternative issues in the hope of an ultimate unity of persons in fellowship, which gives meaning to human effort . . ."[5] The story of the indigo buntings suggests that the theistic alternative offers the most truth because it points to a wide fellowship in eternal life and therefore confirms God's personal nature and concern for all selves.

2. Sheean, *The Indigo Bunting*, 31.
3. Ibid., 31.
4. Ibid., 32.
5. Macmurray, *The Self As Agent*, 222.

Part 4

Dwelling in God

12

Be Still

ON THE FIRST DAY of the course "Theology of Contemplative Prayer," Fr. John O'Donnell, SJ, asked each of us for our definition of prayer. My response was that prayer is to be still and know that God is God. Of course, as a child I would not have put it that way, but basically, this definition has been a constant. Throughout life peace and a sense of divine presence has come to me in nature, beauty, color, light, and above all in silence. My definition of soul is informed by stillness.

Stillroom

The soul is stillness
in the core of flux
where essentials rest
and is no less than
our honored best
and maybe more.

In times of contemplation God has given me perspective and rest in sacramental beauty. I draw from my essay of 1985 that was published in the *Gloucester Daily Times* of Gloucester, Massachusetts, and a poem of 2006, "Haiku Trilogy," which was published in the *Record-Journal* of Meriden, Connecticut.

OTHER ROCKS, OTHER COLORS

I value Rockport rocks—the jagged coastlines, stone walls, and pasture boulders. Still, when my family and I travelled to Arizona, I went in search of other colors and rocks.

The Painted Desert, with mounds of hard, cracked, clay-like sand, was alive with flowing color—rust, tan, gray. I savored the simplicity of sand and grass. Dark rain clouds created a brooding atmosphere. In the distance rays of sun, filtered through rain clouds, turned patches of sky purple.

While entering the silent desert was akin to contemplation in the simplest Congregational meeting house or perhaps a monastery, looking at the Grand Canyon felt like being in a great cathedral. When we pulled up in the car for our first view of the Grand Canyon from the South Rim, we were speechless. Looking at miles of brown, tan, vermillion cliffs, layer upon layer; depth upon depth, we sensed sacred space.

Wildlife in the foreground asked to be acknowledged, too. A friendly squirrel came close. A scrub jay, lighter and more solid blue than his Massachusetts cousins, showed off in a pine tree. Two lizards scampered along the path.

We hiked on the North Rim. Sunlight brought the earth colors of the canyon to life. Enormous rain clouds cast gray shadows on the canyon walls. Sometimes the trail on the top of the canyon was on the edge of a cliff, but the path also led through forest clearings. Shy black Kaibab squirrels with white tails played in the meadows filled with brightly colored wildflowers.

Just outside our log cabin, I sat on a fat cushion of pine needles, looked, and contemplated. The Grand Canyon was formed over many eons. Such immense time put people, plans, and myself into perspective. I was part of the picture, although a tiny part. I felt no one would ever again be able to hassle me for being slow moving or press me into a bigger project than I feel is the right size for me.

We saw beauty that settles within and ripens with joy. In a children's story, *Brighty of the Grand Canyon,* by Marguerite Henry, the burro is a symbol of a joyous way of life. I bought a tiny pewter burro and reaffirmed a promise to cherish the joyful moments, which come to me when striving is balanced with play, which gives life color.

Haiku Trilogy

Zion
Virgin River walk:
Cold water, smooth stones and I
smile from inner life.
North Rim—Grand Canyon
Tears of solemn joy:
Rust and green cliffs plunge into
canyon and my heart.

Bryce:
Vermont fall maples
in hoodoos and pinnacles,
deepest turquoise sky.

Being still is natural for me. Once a friend said that she likes quiet but our home can be too quiet. Maybe so, maybe not so, but in any case, her feelings make a point. Because quiet and often solitude are my style and choice, designing a Sunday school class based on quiet came to me naturally. While I have written and taught my own more academic courses for children, my *Quiet Days* course of 1981 was the most appreciated. This gratitude suggests to me that there is a hunger for quietness. I share my course because my readers may want to do something like it. For starters, it was not literally Sunday school or all day because we met on Friday afternoons after school. My overall purpose was to provide experiences of quiet activity, prayer, meditation, and reflection for girls from our church school in third and fourth grades. I simply said to the girls that our plan was to enjoy a quiet, relaxing time together. We always had a fire in the fireplace and started with a snack. We had five sessions and then, as agreed upon, I offered an option to do another five, which we did. The girls begged for two more, and I agreed but probably should have stopped at ten because the extra two sessions interfered with one family's outing.

The basic format was: 1. Snack—which was always English muffins with butter and a cinnamon and sugar mixture. I cannot remember what we had to drink, but it was likely cocoa. 2. Love circle—we relaxed in our circle on the floor by pretending we were Raggedy Ann dolls. Although I explained the process of meditating with a simple phrase or mantra, I did not have the girls mediate with mantra because I knew that one girl who had the coordination difficulties that I had at her age would just go limp as I can still do. We shared thoughts, feelings, and prayers. I read short, reflective children's stories, many of which are not just for children.

The books that I chose were not explicitly religious, but I often tied them to a biblical passage or found religious implications. Here is a sampling. When we discussed the classic *Hailstones and Halibut Bones* by Mary O'Neill and illustrated by Leonard Weisgard, we talked about our favorite colors and what they mean to us. In a similar vein, Leo Lionni's *Frederick* helped us consider the process of writing poetry. His book *The Biggest House in the World* led us to consider how to keep life simple and how to avoid greed of wanting more than we need. After reading *Prayers from the Ark,* written by Carmen Bernos De Gasztold and translated by Rumer Godden and illustrated by Jean Primrose, we identified the animals that best expressed our own feelings and prayers. About a decade earlier I used this same book with adult women in the Women's Fellowship of the First Congregational Church of Walpole, New Hampshire. This book touched both third graders and people nearing age eighty-three. *In A Spring Garden* edited by Richard Lewis with pictures by Ezra Jack Keats helped us to focus on nature and see how haiku poets and the illustrator celebrate nature in thoughtful word and pictorial images. Finally, *Ox-Cart Man* by Donald Hall with pictures by Barbara Cooney invited reflection on the changing seasons in New England and the rhythm of work and rest. We then talked about rest as a wise aspect of living that was established in the beginning of creation as told in the creation story of Genesis 1—2:3.

3. Embroidery—our craft project was always embroidery. The embroidery stitches that we used were the split stitch, satin stitch, chain stitch, lazy daisy stitch, and cross stitch. We embroidered *God Is Love* in cross stitch. We may have used two or three strands of embroidery floss or we may have used a single strand of crewel yarn as we did for the other projects. Certainly there are more technological ways to make the design today, but at the time I used graph paper to make the words and then traced the design with pencil onto unbleached muslin by taping pattern and cloth to the window. A fish in a combination of stitches on burlap was the least popular because the fabric was scratchy. The most memorable was a red heart in satin stitch on a pillow about six inches square. The satin stitches were long, but as one mother said, "I would never have done it that way, but it worked!" Although I did not stress cooperation over competiveness, the girls did become cooperative with one another. Did quiet reflective time encourage mutual support? I do not know yet suspect that it helped.

To my mind one does not need a retreat or even large margins of time to be still and know that God is. There are, of course, many retreats that are wonderful, and I enjoy reading about them. Often they involve driving skills to get there and at least an average amount of physical stamina. I went on a local retreat where participants walked in a moving prayer circle. Someone said, "Aren't we supposed to move more in synch?" Yes, I was not coordinated enough for a moving prayer circle. Retreats are not always appropriate or doable.

For years I have thought that perhaps it is necessary to have my quiet writing and painting life in order to be still and know that God is. Not so. It took a horrible experience when I did not have time to tie my sneakers that I learned that even seconds of silence saying, "Be still God is," offer sustenance. My husband Ernie constantly fell and hallucinated. His reading level went to below third grade. This went on intensely for over a month after a year of gradual decline. He had occupational therapy that included suggestions to use a weighted cup and heavier utensils when he should have had blood tests instead. In addition to having to be assertive with doctors, I had to deal with an insurance nightmare.

My sister Rosemary, who is on the Rockport ambulance crew, was horrified that his neurologist did not admit him to the hospital after he did poorly on a dementia workup and had to be wheeled into the office so he would not fall down. She said that I fell through the cracks and it is surprising how many people do. Rosemary and her friend Jane, who is also on the ambulance crew and is an emergency room nurse in two hospitals, got things moving in the right direction. Jane came to our home wearing her ambulance jacket, put Ernie into her car, and drove us to the hospital. She then put Ernie into a wheelchair and took him into the emergency waiting room and said, *"Evaluate him!"* They did. To fast forward to the point, Ernie was in the hospital for two weeks so that medicines for tremor and nervousness that had metabolized into Phenobarbital and ammonia could be cleaned out of his system. In short, because doctors did not pay enough attention to how their various prescriptions could interact, he was poisoned and drugged. He cannot remember much of all that happened. Ernie mended but needs to walk with a cane. He has better medicine and a new lease on life.

There were lessons in this ordeal about helpers and silence. Of course I know that helpers can be very different from one another. Yet that truth became even clearer. In addition to Jane and Rosemary, Sally and Gay turned up at just the right time to help me out when I sorely needed them. Sarah, or Sally, as she was called in high school, is now a retired Unitarian-Universalist minister. Gay, whom you met in the last chapter, is far more orthodox in her faith than is Sally. She was a former parishioner who befriended us when Ernie was in the process of leaving the parish ministry and turned up to help us again. Of course, there was also cousin Ted who took our trash to the dump in his ecologically conscious biodiesel fueled Hummer. He cares for creation as a humanist and leads nature walks that give people rest and recreation. Women friends, Ann, Barbara, Carol, Jocelyn, Pat, Robina, and Ruth also helped from afar with cards, handwritten notes, and especially sensitive e-mails. As I said to Rosemary, if I had a party for all the people who helped me, it would be a really strange party!

Helpful people who themselves are signs that God is and silent repetition of belief that God is steered me through the stress. To reiterate, I learned that saying in my mind, "Be still. God is," helped me keep going and that a few seconds of silence can suffice. I believe that being quiet invites God's presence and peace that infuses personal interiors.

Infusion

Hydrangeas bowed their
pink-blue heads when a
snail friend came to call.
The sun shone through
his moonstone shell,
illuminated leaf.
Enter quietly interiority.
Reception is in
Revelation Hall.

When a crisis is not at hand, listen and look. In music you may hear a tone that releases intimations of transcendence. Colors in nature or art may bring consciousness of communion with fellow creatures and the Creator. Experiencing beauty, whether the form is geometric art with perfect proportions or craggy, strange, and wild landscapes, furthers convictions that finite humans are made for infinity. For Christians, affirming incarnate personal love wrought in the passion of Jesus the Christ is certainty of transcendent good will. Be still and in time you may receive the glue of faith, which is the felt knowledge that "underneath are the everlasting arms" and the promise that "joy comes with the morning" (Deut 33:27 RSV; Ps 30:5).

13

Social Action in the Swap Shop

After feeling God's presence in silence, desire for God blossoms into hope to do something for God and for people. Silence flows into service. It must be acknowledged that some people serve others without explicit belief in God, although they too may be sustained by quiet moments and then go forth to help. In any case, tasks are as varied as people. As Ralph Waldo Emerson wrote, "Farmers will give corn; poets will sing; women will sew; laborers will lend a hand; the children will bring flowers."[1] The apostle Paul understood how different individual ways of service can be when he wrote about the variety of gifts in the church bonded together by sharing the same spirit (Rom 12:4–31). One need not be a church member to appreciate his wisdom and the centrality of love that follows in chapter 13. This love in New Testament Greek is *agape,* which means an inclusive form of love and concern for all people in contrast to *eros,* which is romantic love and *philia,* which is friendship.

I am aware that there are many people who do more for others every day than do I. Consider Jane, who works twelve-hour shifts in the emergency rooms of two hospitals and then serves on the volunteer ambulance crew, and my sister, Rosemary, who is a harbormaster and also is an EMT on the ambulance crew. Then there are countless others who work for peace and justice on boards and committees or serve meals in soup kitchens. Service that requires energy is sorely needed. If everyone was like Emily Dickinson or St. Therese, the little flower, or me, no one would call a church synod or even organize a church supper!

Yet little things given by people of great physical strength or more likely almost none at all do also matter. Notes of understanding like the ones I received from my friends from afar when my husband was in the

1. Emerson, *The Selected Writings of Ralph Waldo Emerson*, 193.

hospital gave loving support. These little offerings are ways of giving back to life. Although the little acts of service and love may not be highly visible, we of little strength also serve by praying or knitting prayer shawls or creating in solitude. Understanding art and writing as service, even as a tiny contribution, is very difficult, especially in unpublished or unrecognized years. To my mind, for artists service means using up all your crayons. As Ralph Waldo Emerson wrote, "The talent is the call."[2] Share talent, because not sharing the talent is hoarding gifts.

Truth may be dialectical, maybe even contradictory. There is widespread ecumenical sentiment that people are God's hands and feet. There is huge biblical precedent for service. Yet in order for people, whether poets or medical missionaries, to truly feel that rest is a good thing, it is necessary to consider counterbalancing claims. Whatever our service is to others, a helpful image is being God's jewelry. Jewelry is a nice accessory but not absolutely necessary. This image helps us not to be too impressed with ourselves, as if God could never do without us. "The God who made the world and everything in it, he who is Lord of heaven and earth, does not live in shrines made by human hands, nor is he served by human hands, as though he needed anything, since he himself gives to all mortals life and breath and all things" (Acts 17:24–25). People may benefit from my book, but God already knows that God is. Perhaps I will add a bit of sparkle to the arguments for the existence of God. Yet the assignment to write was God's gift to me because the task was meaningful.

There is a Swap Shop at the Rockport Transfer Station where people leave things that they do not need and take what they can use. Sometimes people also swap ideas in conversations and through the books they leave there. For me the Swap Shop serves as an architectural metaphor for recycling resources and also for the exchange of ideas and theologies. People in the world, which is increasingly a global community, need to grow in awareness of the concerns and thoughts of other people. In a world of dwindling resources and friction among differing faiths, one moral imperative is *save and share.*

2. Ibid., 195.

Freebie

In case future
cultural historians
want to know,
Ernie found a book
  of postcards with
Frank Lloyd Wright's
architectural drawings
in the Swap Shop at
the Rockport Dump.
(Excuse me, Transfer
Station.)
Might as well use them.
Saving and sharing are
support beams of a
re-cycling design—
assigned by community.

The grace inherent in this assignment will surely be surprising signs that God is. Keep one another posted.

Conclusion

Room for Mystery

Many years ago when I was a special student at Andover Newton Theological School, I sat down at a lunch table and a man named Joshua asked to join me. I asked about his life and how he came to be a student at Andover Newton. He was glad to talk and spoke of his journey. He felt called to the ministry late in life. Studying and serving meant that he did not do as much with his family's dry cleaning business as he had previously done. At first his wife was upset. Graduate school is costly. Yet things worked out for all. Joshua told me that after the struggle, the fun part was watching how God worked things out. I truly believe that somewhere today a church has an outstanding pastor named Joshua.

Joshua stopped talking and then said, "I don't even know your name and I have told you so many things." I replied, "I'm Sharon, but what matters most right now is your story." Since I was not at all sure where my theological education would take me, Joshua's insistence that the fun part would come when I could sit back and see how God would makes things happen was reassuring news. We finished lunch and went to different courses. For whatever reasons, we did not meet again. Sometimes God's timing means people must be patient although diligent in pursuit of goals. Now Joshua's prediction is coming true as my publications that contribute to religious education add up. As it is written: "Hope deferred makes the heart sick, but a desire fulfilled is a tree of life" (Prov 13:12).

I have another tale that is worth telling. When I was collecting stories of my contemporaries who had lost their mothers, Margaret, who was elderly at the time, told her story. As a young girl she lived in Walpole, New Hampshire, and was a member of the First Congregational Church that Ernie and I served for six years. She told me that as you get older you are less and less certain and more and more open. As a college student at Boston University she worshipped at the Methodist Church with college friends, as I also worshipped in the Methodist Church on Albion's campus with Barbara, my roommate. Margaret became more and more open to other religions and different Protestant traditions, although as she said, "I always return to Congregationalism."

Then a very different person from a very different faith community said essentially the same thing. During the Ignatian course after I told Margaret's story, Fr. Brian O. McDermott said that as you get older you can become less and less sure. So when I took a course at Yale Divinity School about problems in biblical theology, I told Dr. Leander E. Keck, Dr. Christopher R. Seitz, and my classmates how the thoughts of Margaret and Professor McDermott converged. I mentioned to Dr. Keck that he is no spring chicken and asked how he saw things as he aged. In summary, he said that he is less cockeyed sure but more and more certain about the basics like the love of his parents and the love of God. He said that as long as he could sing "How Great Thou Art," things were all right.

What then is my conclusion? Life sometimes has a way of working out. Caring people help. Loss invites yearning for God. At Weston Jesuit School of Theology, I grew in conviction that there is maternal love in God's heart. In my best moments I feel that ultimately the universe is friendly and there is transcendent good will. Trust and work are basic aspects of living faithfully.

Ultimately God may not need people. Yet in the meantime, people are called to be God's helpers. It is time to add signet ring to the job description of friends of God. People doing their best in large or small ways to befriend people can be God's jewelry, a sign that God is God and loves. The image of being God's signet ring gives me the sustenance of symbol and the power of poetry that propels me forth on my artistic journey. My hope is that this image will also cheer others on their pathways. Then we can sing in one accord, "How Great Thou Art." To believe most certainly through every moment of life in the love of a personal God would be greatest clarity. Yet even the possibility of affinity with loving kindness is uplifting, for love like God is great and dwells in beauty's mystery.

Bibliography

Bailey, James L., and Kyle D. Vander Broek. *Literary Forms in the New Testament: A Handbook.* Louisville, KY: Westminster/John Knox Press, 1992.

Balentine, Samuel E. *Prayer in the Hebrew Bible: The Drama of Divine-Human Dialogue.* Minneapolis, MN: Augsburg Fortress Press, 1993.

Bainton, Roland H. *Here I Stand: A Life of Martin Luther.* Nashville, TN: Abingdon Press, 1978.

Beckett, Sister Wendy. *Sister Wendy's Odyssey: A Journey of Artistic Discovery.* New York: Stewart, Tabori & Chang, 1998.

Bellido, Ramon Tio. *Kandinsky.* Translated by Jane Brenton. New York: Crown, 1988.

Bernos De Gasztold, Carmen. *Prayers from the Ark.* Translated by Rumer Godden and illustrated by Jean Primrose. New York: The Viking Press, 1962.

Book of Common Prayer. New York, NY: Church Publishing, 1979.

Caird, G. B. *The Language and Imagery of the Bible.* Philadelphia, PA: The Westminster Press, 1980.

Cameron, P. S. "Lead Us Not into Temptation." *The Expository Times* 101 (10, 1990) 299–301.

Chace, Sharon R. *An Artistic Approach to New Testament Literature.* Eugene, OR: Wipf and Stock, 2008.

———. *Portfolio of Painterly Poems: A Pilgrim's Path to God.* Eugene, OR: Wipf and Stock, 2006.

———. *When Baby Jesus Grows Up: A Children's Christmas Program.* Lima, OH: CSS Publishing Company, 1998.

Cusson, S.J., Gilles. *Biblical Theology and the Spiritual Exercises: A Method Toward a Personal Experience of God as Accomplishing Within Us His Plan of Salvation.* Translated by Mary Angela Roduit, RC, and George E. Ganss, SJ. St. Louis, MO: The Institute of Jesuit Sources, 1988.

Daziel, Bradford Dudley, ed. *Sarton Selected: An Anthology of the Journals, Novels, and Poems of May Sarton.* Edited with an introduction and notes by Braford Dudley Daziel. New York: W. W. Norton & Company, 1991.

Emerson, Ralph Waldo. *The Selected Writings of Ralph Waldo Emerson.* Introduction by Brooks Atkinson. New York: Random House, 1950.

Farley, Edward. *Faith and Beauty: A Theological Aesthetic.* Burlington, VT: Ashgate Publishing Company, 2001.

Fox, Matthew, Ed. *Hildegaard of Bingen's Book of Divine Works with Letters and Songs.* Santa Fe, NM: Bear & Company, 1987.

Ganss, S. J., George E. *The Spiritual Exercises of Saint Ignatius: A Translation and Commentary by George E. Ganss, SJ.* Chicago: Loyola University Press, 1992.

Grieb, A. Katherine "Living By The Word." *The Christian Century* (June 3, 2008) 20.

Hall, Donald. *Ox-Cart Man*. Illustrated by Barbara Cooney New York: The Viking Press, 1979.

Harrington, S. J., Daniel J. *Who is Jesus? Why is He Important?* Franklin, WI: Sheed & Ward, 1999.

Henry, Marguerite. *Brighty of the Grand Canyon*. Illustrated by Wesley Dennis. New York: Simon & Schuster, 1981

Irwin, Eleanor. *Colour Terms in Greek Poetry*. Toronto, Canada: Hakkert, 1974.

Kandinsky, Wassily. *Concerning the Spiritual in Art*. Translated with an introduction by M. T. H. Sadler. New York: Dover Publications, Inc. 1977.

Keenan, SJ, James F. "Charity, the Mother of the Virtues." *Church* 10.4 (1994) 41–2.

Keller, Werner. *The Bible as History: A Confirmation of the Book of Books*. New York: William Marrow and Company, 1956.

Kittel, Gerhard, ed. *Theological Dictionary of the New Testament. Vol. III*. Translated by Geoffrey W. Bromiley. Grand Rapids, MI: WM.B Eerdmans Publishing Company, 1965.

Kugel, James L. ed. *Poetry and Prophecy: The Beginnings of a Literary Tradition*. Ithaca, NY: Cornell University Press, 1990.

Richard. Lewis, ed. *In A Spring Garden*. Illustrated by Ezra Jack Keats. New York: The Dial Press, 1965.

Liddell and Scott. *A Lexicon: Abridged from Liddell and Scott's Greek-English Lexicon*. Oxford: Oxford University Press, 1963.

Linscott, Robert N. ed. *Selected Poems & Letters of Emily Dickinson*. Garden City, NY: Doubleday & Company, Inc., 1959.

Lionni, Leo. *The Biggest House in the World:* New York: Pantheon Books, 1968.

———. *Frederick*. New York: Pantheon Books, 1967.

Macmurray, John. *The Self as Agent*. Amherst, NY: Humanity Books, 1957.

Marty, Martin E. *A Cry of Absence: Reflections for the Winter of the Heart*. New York: Harper & Row Publishers, 1983.

———. "A Profile of Norman Lear: Another Pilgrim's Progress." *The Christian Century* (January 21, 1987) 55–58.

Meeks, Wayne A., et al., general editors. *The HarperCollins Study Bible: New Revised Standard Version, with the Apocrypha/Deuterocanoincal Books*. New York: Harper Collins, 1993.

Meissner, SJ, MD, W. W. *Ignatius of Loyola: The Psychology of a Saint*. New Haven, CT: Yale University Press, 1992.

O'Malley, John W. *Trent and All That: Renaming Catholicism in the Early Modern Era*. Cambridge, MA: Harvard University Press, 2000.

———. *What Happened At Vatican II*. Cambridge, MA: Harvard University Press, 2008.

O'Neill, Mary. *Hailstones and Halibut Bones: Adventures in Color*. Illustrated by Leonord Weisgard. Garden City, NY: Doubleday & Company, Inc., 1961.

Overy, Paul. *Kandinsky: The Language of the Eye*. New York: Prager Publishers, 1969.

Pilgrim Hymnal, Boston, MA: The Pilgrim Press, 1958.

Ruether, Rosemary Radford, and Rosemary Skinner Keller, general editors. *Women & Religion in America: Volume 2: The Colonial and Revolutionary Periods* New York: Harper & Row, Publishers, San Francisco, 1983.

Selement, George, and Bruce C. Wooley, editors. *Thomas Shepard's Confessions*. Boston, MA: The Colonial Society of Massachusetts, 1981. Collections Vol. 58.

Sheean, Vincent. *The Indigo Bunting: A Memoir of Edna St. Vincent Millay*. New York: Schocken Books, 1973.

Sherry, Patrick. *Spirit and Beauty: An Introduction to Theological Aesthetics. Second edition.* London: SCM Press, 2002.

Snyder, James. *Medieval Art: Painting. Sculpture. Architecture 4th–14th Century.* Englewood Cliffs, NJ: Prentice Hall, Inc. 1989.

Tillich, Paul. *Dynamics of Faith.* New York: Harper & Brothers, 1957.

Tsanoff, Radoslav A. *The Great Philosophers: Second Edition.* New York: Harper & Row, Publishers, 1964.

Underhill, Evelyn. *Practical Mysticism.* Eugene, OR: Wipf and Stock Publishers, 2002.

Whallon, William. *Formula, Character, and Context: Studies in Homeric, Old English, and Old Testament Poetry.* Washington DC: Center for Hellenic Studies, 1969.

Whitford, Frank. *Kandinsky: Watercolours and other Works on Paper.* New York: Thames and Hundson Ind., 1999.

Wilder, Amos N. *The Language of the Gospel: Early Christian Rhetoric.* New York: Harper & Row Publishers, 1964.

Zerwick, S. J., Max, and Mary A. Grosvenor. *A Grammatical Analysis of the Greek New Testament—Unabridged, 4th Revised Edition.* Rome: Editrice Pontificio Istituto Biblico, 1993.

www.ingramcontent.com/pod-product-compliance
Lightning Source LLC
LaVergne TN
LVHW020638100826
845148LV00012B/2235

* 9 7 8 1 6 0 6 0 8 7 0 5 3 *